CODES AND CIPHERS

ALEXANDER d'AGAPEYEFF

Copyright © 2013 Read Books Ltd.
This book is copyright and may not be
reproduced or copied in any way without
the express permission of the publisher in writing

British Library Cataloguing-in-Publication Data
A catalogue record for this book is available from the
British Library

Alexander D'Agapeyeff

Alexander D'Agapeyeff was a Russian-born, English cryptographer and cartographer. He was famous for penning an elementary book on cryptography (the conversion of information from a readable state to apparent nonsense), entitled *Codes and Ciphers,* which was published in 1939. The reason this otherwise conventional book has become so well known, is that it includes an as-yet unbroken cipher. Offered as a 'challenge cipher' at the end of the book, introduced with the words; 'here is a cryptogram upon which the reader is invited to test his skill', D'Agapeyeff's work has never been solved. The code was not included in later editions of the text, and D'Agapeyeff is said to have later admitted to having forgotten how he encrypted it. It is now often found alongside the *Voynich Manuscript* on lists of 'all-time' cipher enigmas. D'Agapeyeff also founded the *Computer Analysts and Programmers Group* (CAP) in May 1962, alongside Barney Gibbens and Harry Baecker. He served as its chairman for the next twenty years. The CAP group initially worked on compilers and system software, and D'Agapeyeff coined the term 'middleware' to describe the interface between application and system software, at a presentation to a NATO conference in 1968. The company subsequently grew to be one of the foremost information technology corporations in the UK, before it merged with the French company *Sema Metra* in 1988.

D'Agapeyeff's famous cipher-text reads:

75628 28591 62916 48164 91748 58464 74748 28483 81638 18174
74826 26475 83828 49175 74658 37575 75936 36565 81638 17585
75756 46282 92857 46382 75748 38165 81848 56485 64858 56382
72628 36281 81728 16463 75828 16483 63828 58163 63630 47481
91918 46385 84656 48565 62946 26285 91859 17491 72756 46575
71658 36264 74818 28462 82649 18193 65626 48484 91838 57491
81657 27483 83858 28364 62726 26562 83759 27263 82827 27283
82858 47582 81837 28462 82837 58164 75748 58162 92000

Can you solve it?

CONTENTS

Chapter		Page
I.	THE BEGINNINGS OF CRYPTOGRAPHY	7
II.	FROM THE MIDDLE AGES ONWARDS	22
III.	SIGNALS, SIGNS, AND SECRET LANGUAGES	48
IV.	COMMERCIAL CODES	70
V.	MILITARY CODES AND CIPHERS	89
VI.	TYPES OF CODES AND CIPHERS	103
VII.	METHODS OF DECIPHERING	121
	BIBLIOGRAPHY	145
	INDEX	147

I want to thank Geoffrey and Marjory Cass who not only encouraged me by showing interest in my writing, but who also found some material which proved very valuable.

And especially I want to express my gratitude to Rachel Wood, without whose help in research and constant co-operation throughout, this book would never have been written.

ALEXANDER D'AGAPEYEFF

CHAPTER I

THE BEGINNINGS OF CRYPTOGRAPHY

'A man is born without any languages and yet is capable of all.'
                                            BISHOP WILKINS

CODES and ciphers appear at first sight to be such complicated and difficult affairs, and so completely wrapped in mystery, that all but the boldest hesitate to tackle them; yet as Bishop Wilkins implied in the sentence quoted above, any person of average ability is capable of acquiring a knowledge of almost any subject, and there is no reason why we should not, with the exercise of patience and perseverance, become familiar with the main principles of Cryptography—to give this fascinating science its proper name.

Most people have a natural curiosity to know what lies beyond the closed door, what secrets are hidden behind signs and symbols that have no obvious meaning. When the urge to solve such problems becomes a dominating force in a man's life, then he may discover new worlds. It may be that there is nothing much left to be discovered in the material world, but there are unlimited possibilities in the world of thoughts and ideas.

But thought, if it is to be effective, must be controlled and disciplined, and a knowledge of codes and ciphers can only be acquired by means of orderly and patient thinking. The same habit of thought is of incalculable value in many walks of life, so what is taken up as a hobby and amusement may be a training for more serious things.

The history of cryptography is very old—almost as old as writing itself. In the library of the British Museum and elsewhere there are books on the subject written hundreds of years ago by men whose names are forgotten but whose orderly precision of thought provides us with a basis for practically every cipher we now use.

Cryptography itself dates back to the oldest scriptures and fables that have come down to us, and it was closely related to the earliest attempts at writing.

'The noblest acquisition of mankind is speech,' wrote Astles in the last century, 'and the most useful is writing. The first eminently distinguishes man from the brute creation, and the second from uncivilised savages.'

The oldest scripture of India, the *Vedas*, claims that Brahma himself first communicated letters to mankind. We find also that the great Greek philosopher Plato attributed the invention of letters to the god Zeus (Theuth), while another assumed that Hermes (called by the Egyptians Thoth) taught letters to man.

The first mention of letters in our Bible occurs in Exodus xvii. 14: 'And the Lord said unto Moses, Write this for a memorial in a book . . .' This passage gave rise to a discussion whether it was God who gave letters to Moses, or whether Moses already knew how to write.

However, all these legends show very clearly the value that mankind placed on the art of letters. Otherwise it is unlikely that these different scriptures of various races, separated from each other both in time and in space, would have attributed, even indirectly, the invention of writing to divine powers.

In the olden days secret writing was not so necessary as it is to-day, as very few people could read or write, and doubtless at first it was only a few priests and scholars who used it.

We know that even in the early days of Egypt there already existed, apart from hieroglyphs, two kinds of writing; the hieratic or sacred writing, used secretly by the

THE BEGINNINGS OF CRYPTOGRAPHY 9

priests, and the demotic or vulgar writing, used by the people. The former writing was at all times guarded from the people, and it is recorded that one of the Pharaohs found it necessary to issue an order forbidding the priests to teach the secret letters to the ordinary citizen.

Plutarch mentions a 'famous inscription' on an obelisk outside a temple at Saïs, dedicated, he says, to Minerva; on this were painted an infant, an old man, a hawk, a fish, and a 'sea-horse' which was the name given to hippos by the Ancient Greeks. The meaning of these figures, he thought, was that young and old know that God hates impudence. An eighteenth-century author translated this differently. 'The infant, which is the first figure, represents man's first entrance into the world, and the old man implies the going out of it; the falcon represents God; the fish, hatred, because of its association with the hated sea, which symbolised storms; and the sea-horse, murder, violence and injustice, because by ancient fables the sea-horse murdered its own sire when it became of age.' The meaning he says may be: 'O you that enter the world and go out of it, know that God hates injustice!'

Apropos of this story, I have found in Pietri Valeriano's 1575 edition of *Hieroglyphica* a drawing supposedly illustrating the obelisk described by Plutarch. It is reproduced here. The fact that Plutarch calls it an obelisk may indicate that there was some traditional Egyptian story connected with it, and perhaps he based his version on an eyewitness's account.

However that may be, the details on the obelisk are quite obviously pure imagination. Plutarch says himself that it was found on a temple at Saïs, but later authors, copying this passage from his works, for some reason mention Thebes. Saïs, however, was under the Nile mud in Plutarch's time, so that he could never have seen the original inscription. At Thebes nothing of the kind has ever been found.

Plutarch himself did not know how to read hieroglyphs; the conventionalized part of them would have no meaning for him, for by his time all knowledge of hieroglyphs was already lost. And if some traveller had ever seen or copied some kind of an inscription Plutarch would recognize only a part of it. In such an hieroglyph as this:

(meaning 'upon the') he would recognize only the child's head, and in this:

(meaning 'head' or 'god') he would understand only that it was an old man because of the beard.

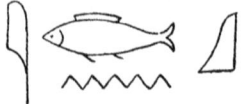

THE BEGINNINGS OF CRYPTOGRAPHY 11

In this inscription (=envelop) the only figure he would recognize would be the fish; while in this:

(which means 'a moment of time') he would see only the hawk and the hippo's head. We now see where Valeriano got his head of a hippopotamus, which led me to try to reconstruct this.

Any attempt to do so, however, is so much of a speculation that, not being an Egyptologist, I had to give it up. But it is quite safe to assume that the inscription (if any) mentioned by Plutarch certainly did not have the meaning ascribed to it. It is also quite clear that the authors who copied Plutarch never tried to verify their facts.

In brief, Plutarch was writing in ignorance.

Symbolism has always been of great influence among Eastern peoples. The sending of a bird, a mouse, a frog and an arrow by the Scythians to the Persians was a gentle hint to them that unless they could escape as birds, could swim as frogs, or conceal themselves as mice, they were hastening to swift destruction.

The necessity of sending messages in a form which could be understood only by a select few was apparently realized very early in history, and it was from this necessity that arose the science of cryptography.

Cryptography (from the Greek *kryptos*, secret, and *graphe*, writing) is a manner of conveying messages in a form which will prevent anybody reading them except those who have the key.

The form used may be a code, i.e., a set of letters or words with arbitrary agreed-upon meanings for brevity or secrecy;

or a cipher (Hebrew *saphar*, to number) meaning secret writing, either in invented characters, or characters given different powers, or even figures with agreed meanings.

Thus, if we agree that we shall use 'Tom' for 'Arriving by the 12 o'clock train tomorrow', and 'Jack' for 'Leaving here by car at 4 p.m. today', this will be a code; while if we agree that the figures 1, 2, 3, 4, . . . stand for a, b, c, d, . . . etc., then 25,5,19 will mean 'yes' and 14,15 will mean 'no', and this will be a cipher.

There are naturally many ways of 'coding' or 'enciphering' a message. Although their employment by armies for military purposes excites the imagination, secret ciphers were used much more in the olden days for teaching secret knowledge, and in later times for political and diplomatic purposes. In modern times they are employed for purposes of trade and commerce.

In this connexion it must be realised that codes are not used in business only for the sake of saving money on telegrams, but also to keep certain information from competitors. In consequence a great many private codes are used.

We find, however, that secret ways of sending messages for peaceful purposes were known at the beginning of civilization. In the Bible both Isaiah and Jeremiah used a form of cipher to hide the real meaning of their prophecies from the Babylonians.

In the Middle Ages a very interesting study was made of what is known as the 'hidden sacred mysteries of the Scriptures'. This study, known as cabbalism, was at that time regarded as almost a science. For instance, in Genesis xlix. 10: 'The sceptre shall not depart from Judah, nor a lawgiver from between his feet, until Shiloh come; and unto him shall the gathering of the people be', the initial letters

THE BEGINNINGS OF CRYPTOGRAPHY 13

of the words: 'until Shiloh come; and unto him shall the gathering of the people be' spell in Hebrew the word 'Jesus'.

In the story of the Creation in Genesis i, in the same manner, the word 'truth' is spelled six times. Also a very important cabbalism occurs in Exodus iii. 13: 'And Moses said unto God, Behold, when I come unto the children of Israel, and shall say unto them, The God of your fathers hath sent me unto you; and they shall say to me, What is his name? What shall I say unto them?' The final letters of the words in the last line of this verse form in Hebrew the word 'Jehovah', which was God's secret name. Julius Caesar used this kind of cipher in his military correspondence, writing 'd' for 'a', 'e' for 'b', etc., and called that *quartam elementorum literam.*

We can be fairly confident in stating that signals for sending messages at a distance were used as long ago as 1184 B.C., and this was quite apart from the legendary use of such signals by Medea in her conspiracy against Jason. Actually the reading of the Trojan war episode makes one believe that some sort of flash or mirror apparatus was used to give the signal to unlock the wooden horse of Troy.

Again, Agamemnon informed Queen Clytemnestra by fire signals that Troy was taken. This is probably the first example of an agreed code.

Some time later the Spartans during their wars used a form of staff called 'skytale', round which a roll of parchment was wound slantwise. Letters written seemingly at random on the edges of the unrolled parchment could be consecutively read forming complete words when the roll was wound again round another staff of equal diameter, the thickness of the latter giving the necessary distance for the appropriate letters to come together. To us this does not appear a very secret method of writing, as it can be easily deciphered by juggling together the edges of the roll; but doubtless at the time of Alcibiades and Lysander, when the invention was new, knowledge of reading was sufficiently rare to ensure the secrecy of the 'skytale' method.

Skytale

In those early days many strange and often cruel methods of sending secret messages were employed. A certain Histiaeus, Greek ambassador in Persia, wishing to send secret political information to his country, shaved a slave's head, and under pretext of curing his bad eyes, branded a message on his skull, let the hair grow again, and sent him to Greece, telling him that when Aristagoras shaved his head the second time his eyes would recover. Others used to drug their slaves and brand messages on their backs, and when they came to they were sent to their destination, having been told that when they arrived and uncovered their backs a healing ointment would be given to them. In both cases the slaves knew nothing about the important messages they were carrying.

Tacitus describes several ways of sending messages into a besieged city, such as using a manuscript instead of a bandage on a wound, sewing a letter in the soles of a person's shoes, rolling thin leaves of lead bearing the written message into ear-rings, and writing on wooden tablets which were then covered with wax. All these, however, were not so much examples of secret writing as of writing carried secretly.

About 350 B.C. the first telegraphic machine was improvised by Aeneas Tacticus. It consisted of a narrow earthen vessel filled with water, which could either be added to or

THE BEGINNINGS OF CRYPTOGRAPHY 15

drawn off at will. A piece of stick was thrust through a cork floating on top of the water, and at the end of the stick was a torch. This stick was marked with notches about three inches apart, and each notch stood for some common event that happens in war.

If water was drawn off from the vessel, the stick would descend by so many divisions, and an observer, noting the distance the stick had travelled, could tell which of the expected events had occurred.

Later Polybius improved on this method by a system of torches together with a special code consisting of five groups of five letters each:

	1	2	3	4	5
1	A	F	K	P	V
2	B	G	L	R	W
3	C	H	M	S	X
4	D	I	N	T	Y
5	E	J	O	U	Z

(Q was purposely omitted to obtain 25 letters only.)

The signaller was provided with ten torches, five for the left hand and five for the right; with the latter he signalled the number of the group, and with the former the letter in this particular group, so that two torches in the right hand meant group No. 2, and four torches in the left hand meant the fourth letter in that group, which is I.

The great advantage of this was that any messages could be sent, and not merely messages that had been pre-arranged, as in the case of the notched stick.

It may surprise some of us to realize how very early this kind of telegraphy was invented; but we find also that at an even earlier date propaganda, which we regard as belonging exclusively to the twentieth century, was used by a Spartan king at the siege of Trezene. He ordered his soldiers to shoot blunted arrows into the town bearing this inscription: 'I come to liberate you.' Reading these signs on the arrows, the discontented inhabitants revolted against their tyrant, and eventually opened their city gates to the Spartans.

A few hundred years later, when the Roman Empire was at its height, a great advance in cryptic writing was made by a freed slave of Cicero's, Tullius Tyro, whose name was immortalized through his invention of the first method of shorthand, in which he used arbitrary marks for whole words. Although some historians say that he only perfected the method which was already known to the poet Ennius, nevertheless the characters used in Germany as late as the tenth century were called Tyronian after him.

In this connexion a curious story is told concerning the discovery of an old psalter inscribed with Tyronian characters, but labelled at the time of Pope Julius II 'Psalterium in lingua Armenica' by some monk who mistook Tyronian characters for Armenian writing.

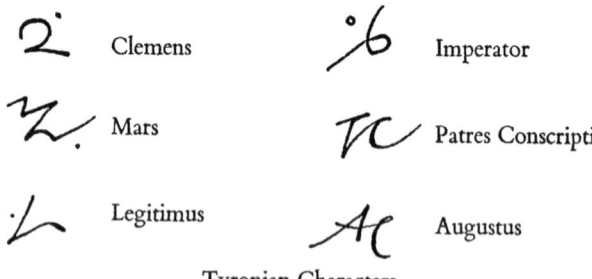

Tyronian Characters

We give a few of these characters, which were non-alphabetical but so well systematized that words beginning or ending similarly had the same kind of marks.

THE BEGINNINGS OF CRYPTOGRAPHY 17

Probably this may have given rise amongst the Romans to the excessive use of abbreviations of words, such as they inscribed on statues, coins, and so on; but this was obviously done not so much for reasons of secrecy as to put the greatest amount of information in the least amount of space. This tradition is still carried on in the present day on our coins: DEI GRA : BRITT : OMN : REX FID : DEF : meaning 'Dei Gratia Britanniae Omnis Rex Fidei Defensor'.

When the art of painting ikons was flourishing in Byzantium, an abbreviated form of writing the names of the saints to whom the ikons were dedicated was employed. In Slavonic Russian, as in Latin, a wavy sign was used over the abbreviated word, thus:

господь (the Lord) is reduced to г︠дь︡.

Doubtless one can trace the origin of these abbreviations to the time when early Christians were persecuted in Rome, and used to hide their votive images from the pagans under incomprehensible marks known only among themselves. Quite possibly this may have been one of the origins of the Orthodox and Roman Catholic custom of making the sign of the cross, which was used as a secret sign to show their adherence to the Christian faith.

It may be that the Fascist salutes, the Communist clenched fist, the Chinese bow and the Mohammedan salaam also belong to the same category.

Another example of the ingenuity of the Romans, at the time of the Roman conquest of Britain, was the building of Hadrian's wall to keep out the savage Picts. It was over a hundred miles long, and watchtowers were placed along it about a mile apart. Inside the thickness of this wall long hollow pipes and trunks were built through which the sentries passed signals to each other by tapping on the hollow

B

tubes and using Polybius' code, or even just shouting into them, the pipes carrying the sounds along to the next tower.

Walchius, a writer in the Middle Ages, pondering on this system of Roman telephony, came to the astonishing conclusion that if words were spoken into a hollow tube which was sealed at one end and then corked at the other, the sound might remain in the tube until it was uncorked again, when the words would flow out in their proper sequence. As far as we know, this notion has never been put into practice. Nevertheless in this story we seem to get a hint of the modern gramophone record.

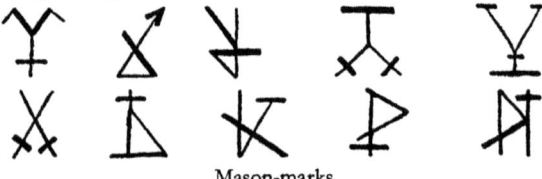

Mason-marks

Another set of secret signs which exercised the curiosity not only of ancient writers but also of some moderns were the so-called mason-marks, found on medieval cathedrals and other contemporary buildings; surprisingly similar marks were found also on the old Egyptian pyramids and temples. We reproduce a few of them here, and although nobody really knows what they mean, it has been suggested that they were the marks of actual individual masons who were paid at piece-work rates. As can be seen, the only rule about them was that they had to be made up of at least one angle. A great many people read into these signs some occult significance or associate them with freemasonry.

Perhaps we may regard trade-marks and hall-marks on silver as the present-day descendants and sole survivors of these ancient mason-marks.

An alphabet called the 'Oghams', based on straight and

THE BEGINNINGS OF CRYPTOGRAPHY

inclined vertical lines, over, under, or through a horizontal line, is supposed to have been used in the pre-Christian era by the Celts; and many stone monuments can be seen in Ireland and Wales bearing these curious incisions. Nobody has hitherto bothered very much about these 'Oghams', but we reproduce a set of them as an example of an invented alphabet which was actually used many centuries ago.

Oghams

In the fifth century the fabulous Pharamond, reputedly 43rd in succession to the even more legendary Marcovir, king of the Franks, was credited with the invention of several secret alphabets. Actually a few of them were used by the great Charlemagne when communicating with the vassal kings of his vast empire. Some of these letters are preserved to this day in Paris. They seem rather uncouth, and as they certainly required a good deal of time to encipher, they were easily misread and were soon given up. The older transposition ciphers, which were used by the Syracusans and Carthaginians, came into general use again for diplomatic and political purposes. Though they were simple, the decline of learning in the dark ages made it less likely that any unauthorized person would try to decipher them.

We come again to the Bible, on which by tradition the first transposition ciphers are based. It is here that the cabbalists read the word 'Sheshach' for 'Babel' (Jeremiah xxv. 26). 'Babel' is written with the second and twelfth letters of the Hebrew alphabet, whilst 'Sheshach' is written with the second and twelfth letters from the end. Isaiah concealed his prophecy from the people (Isaiah vii. 6) by writing 'Tabeal' for (King) 'Remaliah'. This method is called 'Athbash', and the word itself is the key to the kind of transposition used, for 'A' is the first letter of the Hebrew alphabet and 'TH' is the last, while 'B' is the second and 'SH' is the second from the end, etc. There is another kind which is known as 'Albam', where the middle letter 'L' is used instead of the first letter 'A,' and the letter 'M' is used for 'B', etc. Such simple transposition ciphers were used up to the seventeenth century.

These ciphers, however, were so easily read that they were superseded by a totally different kind of secret writing. The work of the alchemist took a practical turn in the invention of so-called sympathetic inks; the old medieval books give full descriptions of various invisible fluids which could only be seen when heat or water was applied to the writing.

We quote several of these recipes, one of which, a solution of CHLORIDE OF COBALT, although it does not make an entirely invisible ink, is yet so pale that no unsuspecting person would notice it on paper. If the paper written on is heated, however, the letters will appear greenish in colour but quite clear. The advantage is that the moment the paper is cold again the writing disappears, and this process can be repeated as often as is necessary.

OIL OF VITRIOL also makes a very good sympathetic ink. The proportions needed are one fluid ounce to a pint of water. On first mixing this, heat is generated, owing to a strong chemical action, and the solution must become perfectly cold again before it can be used. It is not entirely invisible, but if some innocent-looking epistle has dots made over certain letters which convey the secret message, they will be too weak to be noticed. On heating the paper they will be visible.

AQUA FORTIS in the proportions of one part to three parts

of water can be relied upon to make an invisible ink. A solution of alum would also have the same result. Both these inks clearly appear on damping the paper, and the aqua fortis ink disappears again as the paper dries.

In case of emergency, these chemicals may be difficult to get hold of, but there are ordinary household articles that also make excellent invisible inks. The juice of a lemon, of an onion, vinegar or ammonia, used as inks, all remain invisible until they are heated. In the case of the onion juice, however, not only is it uncomfortable to prepare, but if a plain piece of paper reeking of onion fell into the hands of the most unsuspecting person it might easily give the secret away.

Another obsolete method is to incise letters on some soft wood—poplar, for instance—to the depth of a quarter of an inch, and then immediately afterwards either beat the wood with a hammer until the letters can no longer be seen or put it in a vice. To read the message the wood must be damped, and the incised letters will appear again.

CHAPTER II

FROM THE MIDDLE AGES ONWARDS

TOWARDS the end of the fourteenth century Europe was reorganizing itself. The nations started to assume some of the forms we know to-day. There were wars and excursions and a great deal of diplomatic activity, as civilization and learning began to emerge from the chaos of pre-Renaissance. For these reasons the old transposition ciphers, as well as the clumsy methods of invented alphabets, were no longer of much use; they were too easily deciphered and took too long to deal with. There was a need of a more scientific approach to this subject, and out of the art of cryptography man had to evolve the science of codes and ciphers.

At that time all science was more of a mystery than it is to-day. Man had just begun a rational search into the secrets of nature; but that search seemed very close to magic, and it was only the very few enlightened and fearless people who dared to look into the unknown. It is due to the early alchemists that we have our modern chemistry, and to astrologers that we have the science of astronomy.

The first book dealing with cryptology was written in 1499 by John Tritheim, Abbot of Spanheim, a small town in Germany. There is little doubt that Tritheim merely collected the ciphers already used by certain European courts, and as he was familiar with occult matters, he also proposed a kind of first code based on cabbalistic words wherein he tried to hide the real meaning under cover of a mysterious language.

The courts became frightened lest Tritheim in his *Polygraphia*—or as he called it 'a manner of occult writing'—was giving away too much, so they started a campaign of abuse against him, stressing his magic practices; and the leaders of several religious bodies persuaded Frederic II of the Palatinate, who was also interested in these subjects and had the original manuscript in his library, to burn it publicly.

This was done with great pomp and ceremony, and popular feeling was roused to such an extent that it was very lucky for the Abbot that he escaped being burnt as well.

However, the first edition in Latin was printed in 1518, and a French translation was published as early as 1561, by Collange; it was very soon followed by a German translation.

Actually Tritheim, being a Benedictine Abbot, only carried out a Benedictine tradition. This order, in the ninth century, published a *Treatise of Diplomacy* in which they described one of their own ciphers based on replacements of all the vowels by dots, 'i' by one dot, 'a' by two, 'e' by three, 'o' by four, and 'u' by five, so that 'Bonifacia' would read 'B::n.f:c.:'. This idea is obviously not very complicated, and it rather suggests that the Benedictine monks had other ciphers which they preferred not to publish.

The first part of Tritheim's *Polygraphia* consisted of a number of code words for each letter of the alphabet, but arranged in such a manner that if each letter of the message was replaced by a code word, the result was a complete sentence having an innocent meaning.

Below will be found fourteen coded alphabets illustrating the way they were meant to be used:

CODES AND CIPHERS
TRITHEIM'S CODE ALPHABETS

	1st Alphabet	*2nd Alphabet*	*3rd Alphabet*	*4th Alphabet*
A.	Jesus	Immortal	Producing	Angels
B.	God	Omnipotent	Saving	Archangels
C.	Saviour	Compassionate	Illuminating	Saints
D.	King	Ineffable	Conferring	Spheres
E.	Pastor	Universal	Moderating	Heavens
F.	Author	Almighty	Expressing	Sea
G.	Redemptor	Magnificent	Governing	Earth
H.	Prince	Puissant	Disposing (of)	World
I,J.	Maker	Just	Dominating	Men
K.	Conservator	Sempiternal	Creating	Sun
L.	Governor	Celestial	Cognising	Moon
M.	Emperor	Divine	Guiding	All
N.	Moderator	Excellent	Blessing	Hierarchies
O.	Rector	Triumphant	Constituting	Bodies
P.	Judge	Clement	Confirming	Spirits
Q.	Illustrator	Peaceful	Conducting	Souls
R.	Illuminator	Pacific	Sanctifying	Times
S.	Consolator	Invisible	Honouring	Humanity
T.	Sire	Eternal	Ministrating (to)	Ages
U,V,W.	Dominator	Invincible	Exorcising	Eternity
X.	Creator	Benign	Elevating	Firmaments
Y.	Psalmist	Pitiable	Sustaining	Stars
Z.	Sovereign	Incomprehensible	Vivifying	Air
&.	Protector	Excellent	Ordering	Cosmos

	5th Alphabet	*6th Alphabet*	*7th Alphabet*	*8th Alphabet*
A.	Gives	(To the) Christians	Eternal	Life
B.	Delivers	Requiring (needy)	Perpetual	Joy
C.	Attributes	Faithful	Infinite	Joyousness
D.	Increases	Attendants	Angelic	Glory
E.	Presents	Righteous	Immortal	Consolation
F.	Renders	Penitents	Enduring	Felicity
G.	Remits	Good	Incomprehensible	Beatitude
H.	Renders	Supplicants	Incorruptible	Jubilation
I.J.	Envoys	Hopeful	Durable	Tranquillity
K.	Transmits	Patient	Permanent	Amenity
L.	Administers	Afflicted	Ineffable	Recreation
M.	Permits	All	Celestial	Clarity
N.	Inspires	Tormented	Divine	Union
O.	Retributes	Perturbed	Interminable	Peace
P.	Orders	Desolated	Perfect	Light
Q.	Contributes	Mortals	Sincere	Glorification
R.	Frees	Humans	Pure	Benediction

5th Alphabet	6th Alphabet	7th Alphabet	8th Alphabet
S. Confers	Languishing	Glorious	Security
T. Manifests	Repentant	Supernatural	Favours
U,V,W. Reveals	Catholics	Indicible	Fruition
X. Maintains	In the world	Peaceful	Happiness
Y. Admits	Sinners	Happy	Light
Z. Agitates	Charitables	Excellent	Exultation
&. Develops	Virtuous	Uplifting	Pleasures

9th Alphabet	10th Alphabet	11th Alphabet	12th Alphabet
A. (Together with his) Saints	in Heavens	Majesty	Incomprehensible
B. Servants	Ever and ever	Goodness	God
C. Loved	Without end	Kindliness	Creator
D. Saved	In one Infinity	Sapience	Favour
E. Beatified	Perpetuity	Charity	Jesus
F. Elected	Sempiternity	Power	Transformator
G. Confessors	Enduring	Infinity	Dominator
H. Apostles	Incessantly	Sublimity	Preservator
I,J. Evangelists	Irrevisably	Benignity	Immortal
K. Martyrs	Eternally	Commiseration	Supreme
L. Angels	In glory	Excellence	Mighty
M. Archangels	In the light	Pity	Omnipotent
N. Dominions	In Paradise	Clemency	Ineffable
O. Proselytes	Always	Mercy	Redemptor
P. Disciples	In divinity	Divinity	Sempiternal
Q. Deified	In Deity	Deity	Governor
R. Ministers	In felicity	Omnipotence	Rector
S. Sanctified	In his reign	Virtue	Sovereign
T. Predestined	In His Kingdom	Love	Invincible
U,V,W. Preferred	In beatitude	Perfection	Puissant
X. Prophets	In his vision	Force	Merciful
Y. Patriarchs	In his magnificence	Magnificence	All Powerful
Z. Cherubs	To the Throne	Grandeur	Magnificent
&. Professors	In all Eternity	Favour	Sanctified

13th Alphabet	14th Alphabet
A. Sincerely	Preached
B. Really	Announced
C. Saintly	Published
D. Evangelically	Revealed
E. Devotedly	Denounced
F. Intelligibly	Acclaimed
G. Evidently	Exalted
H. Publicly	Sermoned
I, J. Faithfully	Interpreted
K. Ardently	Reported
L. Constantly	Narrated
M. Sagely	Served

CODES AND CIPHERS

13th Alphabet	14th Alphabet
N. Carefully	Praised
O. Virtuously	Recited
P. Catholically	Pronounced
Q. Cordially	Repeated
R. Reverently	Treated
S. Theologically	Speculated
T. Justly	Collated
U,V,W. Divinely	Spread
X. Learnedly	Cognized
Y. Entirely	Recognized
Z. Studiously	Contemplated
&. Spiritually	Produced

Amen

Example:

Plain Text: 'DO NOT USE BEARER.'

Write this, spacing the letters and number them:

```
  D          O         N           O          T
  1          2         3           4          5
(The) King Triumphant Blessing(the) Bodies Manifests(to the)
  U          S         E                      B
  6          7         8                      9
Catholics  Pure    Consolation (together with) His Servants
  E                    A           R          E          R
  10                   11          12         13         14
(in) Perpetuity The Majesty (of the)Rector Devotedly Treated.
AMEN.
```

Look in the first alphabet for the word under 'D' = 'King' which you write under the first letter; look in the second alphabet for the word for 'O' = 'Triumphant', and in the third alphabet for the word for 'N' = 'Blessing', and so on.

The encoded message will read:

'The King Triumphant blessing the Bodies manifests to the Catholics pure consolation together with his Servants in Perpetuity the Majesty of the Rector Devotedly treated. Amen.'

which sounds like a passage from a sermon or an old religious book.

The second part of the Book gave curious occult words

as code words, and the third was just a cabbalistic hotchpotch. But all these parts were interlarded with whole pages hinting at wonderful revelations to be made to those who persevered in studying the mysteries set forth in the book.

Unfortunately for himself, in the last part Tritheim alluded to a number of extraordinary characters which he called 'Spiritus nocturni' and 'diurni', and it was through this that he was accused of practising black magic.

The second part of Tritheim's book contains a great number of substitution alphabets, using numerals ingeniously constructed in the form of disks (his printing costs must have been terrific). These were probably in use at the time and were merely collected. Tritheim seems to have been the first to arrange them systematically.

The unfortunate thing about his codes in the first book is that the coded message requires as many words as there are letters in the plain text, which makes the cryptogram exceedingly long. On the other hand, it is certainly hard to decipher, especially as the alphabets can easily be mixed up, in which case deciphering is almost impossible. The use of a new code word for each letter renders the frequency-table method useless.

The next mention of cryptography occurs in the famous book *De Subtilitate* by Jerome Cardan, who was born in Italy in 1501. Cardan was one of the most erudite and versatile natural philosophers of the Renaissance. By profession a physician, he was learned in all sciences, mathematics, theology, and astrology. His services as a doctor were at one time sought all over Europe by kings, dukes, and cardinals, and he lectured at the Universities of Bologna and Pavia. He achieved notoriety by his casting of the horoscope of Jesus Christ, to do which, in those days, required a good deal of courage as well as an established position.

He invented what is known as the trellis cipher which he himself describes as follows:

'Obtain two identical pieces of parchment and cut holes in them of similar dimensions to the usual size of your letters, some of these to hold seven, three, eight or ten, enough to contain about one hundred and twenty letters in all. One of these parchments you give to your correspondent and the other keep yourself. When you wish to communicate your secret you write what you want, taking care to put down one sentence only on each sheet through the holes on the parchment, and then you must try and compose an innocent-looking message to fill in the gaps. Be careful to avoid any suspicion, and preserve the continuity of your subject throughout the letter. When your friend receives it, all he has to do is to cover the sheet with his second parchment, and your secret message will immediately appear.'

This cipher, in several disguises, has been claimed as a new invention by various ingenious people ever since.

Italy in the sixteenth century was a hot-bed of political intrigue. The Council of Ten, the Borgias, the Visconti, and the Farnese were fighting, spying, poisoning, and scheming in a struggle for power. Obviously they had to communicate with each other secretly, and, as is often the case, the demand created the supply.

An Italian, Giovanni Baptista della Porta, of Naples, also a prolific writer on a variety of subjects covering all the learning of his age, wrote a number of books in which he laid the foundations of a scientific approach to subjects which interest mankind even to-day.

His book on *Human Physiognomy* gave ideas to the Swiss writer Lavater, and in *Human Magic* there are important observations on mirrors and reflections of light rays, etc. He also wrote a volume on ciphers in which he mentions secret communications by means of bells, gestures, signs, torches, and invisible writing, and mentions a variation of the ancient skytale method which is rather ingenious.

Wind a thread round a stick, the threads lying quite close to each other, and then write the secret message in ink across the thread, having first steeped the thread in alum water to prevent the ink from spreading. Then unwind the thread and send it either round a parcel or in a ball to your friend. No one will take notice of the markings on the thread, and only when it is wound round a stick with the same diameter as the original one will the message be read.

Porta also gave a lot of advice on how to decipher secret messages, but nowadays his ideas are of no use. Nevertheless he was the first to point out the frequency of certain vowels, and the importance of differentiating between vowels and consonants, double letters, e.g., ll, tt, cc, etc.; and finally he proposed the use of an alphabet.

ALU	BMX	CNZ
DO	EP	FQ
GR	HS	IT

The nine groups were distinguished by nine fundamental characters, thus

⌐⌐⌐, ⌐⌐⌐, ⌐⌐⌐

These characters stood for the first letters in the groups; the second and third letters were indicated by the addition of dots in the angles of the characters. Thus ⌐˙ = C and ⌐ = N; ⌐ = H, ⌐˙ = S.

This artificial alphabet, with different modifications, was used extensively in Tudor times. Cardinal Wolsey used a modification of it in 1527 when he was English Ambassador in Vienna.

Porta devised yet another cipher, which is one of the most complicated of the early ones. It was probably the first cipher invented with which a key word was used, and this table shows it:

	a	b	c	d	e	f	g	h	i	j	k	l	m
A B	n	o	p	q	r	s	t	u	v	w	x	y	z
C D	z	n	o	p	q	r	s	t	u	v	w	x	y
E F	y	z	n	o	p	q	r	s	t	u	v	w	x
G H	x	y	z	n	o	p	q	r	s	t	u	v	w
I J	w	x	y	z	n	o	p	q	r	s	t	u	v
K L	v	w	x	y	z	n	o	p	q	r	s	t	u
M N	u	v	w	x	y	z	n	o	p	q	r	s	t
O P	t	u	v	w	x	y	z	n	o	p	q	r	s
Q R	s	t	u	v	w	x	y	z	n	o	p	q	r
S T	r	s	t	u	v	w	x	y	z	n	o	p	q
U V	q	r	s	t	u	v	w	x	y	z	n	o	p
W X	p	q	r	s	t	u	v	w	x	y	z	n	o
Y Z	o	p	q	r	s	t	u	v	w	x	y	z	n

Each pair of capitals in the left hand column together control the alphabet ranged in two lines to their right. The keyword is formed from these capitals and its letters in succession indicate the alphabets selected. For instance, to cipher the word 'red' by means of the code word 'car', you find the capital letter 'C' in the left-hand column, and look along the line to the right until you find the small letter 'r'. The ciphered letter is the one that appears above or below this letter—in this case 'f'. Repeat the process with the other two letters and the result is 'frv'.

It stands to reason that to decipher, the same method is adopted. If NOT is the keyword 'vtu' = bad.

Porta suffered almost immediately from a copyist. A French diplomat, Blaise de Vigénère, author of several books on occult subjects as well as an alchemist and astrologer (the usual combination in the sixteenth century), wrote an *Occult Treatise on Letters*, in which, between futile cabbalistic dreams, he mentions a good many of Porta's ideas, though they were not as precisely and clearly expressed as in the Italian book. Nevertheless Vigénère produced an ingenious code, which is very similar to one suggested by Bacon and still used to-day. This is as follows:

1st *Letters* (*Cipher*)

	AA	BB	CC	AB	AC	BC	CB
A	a	d	g	k	o	v	u
B	l	e	h	m	p	s	x
C	c	f	i	n	g	t	z

3rd *Letter* (*Cipher*)

The small letters are the plain text, the capitals the cipher.

To cipher 'the foe', one finds the small letter 't', and writes down first the two capitals in the top horizontal line and then the single capital in the left-hand column; thus 't' = BCC, and 'the foe' = BCC CCB BBB BBC ACA BBB.

For greater secrecy the coded message should be sent in groups of five letters, and should not show the actual length of words as this would help to decipher the message.

Vigénère also arranged a modified version of Porta's multiple alphabet cipher which is given on p. 33. Below is an example showing the use of a code word TROY. The procedure is similar to that used with Porta's table, only each letter of the key word (on the side of the table) gives the entire cipher alphabet, the plain text alphabet being on the first top line (printed in capitals).

Key word : TROY

Message (plain text): 'FOOD SUPPLIES RUNNING OUT'

Keyword :   TROY TROYTROY TROYTRO YTR

Message written
for enciphering :   FOOD SUPPLIES RUNNING OUT

Cipher :   AGDB NNENFBSQ MNCLDFU MPM

Cryptogram : AGDBN NENFB SQMNC LDFUM PMZYX

Almost at the same time a noble duke—the Duke of Brunswick-Luneburg—entered the field of secret writing, and he published a book called *Cryptographiae* under the pseudonym of Gustavus Selenus. This was in itself a cryptogram: SELENE means 'moon' in Greek and Luneburg means 'moontown', while Gustavus was an anagram of his Christian name, Augustus.

	A	B	C	D	E	F	G	H	IJ	K	L	M	N	O	P	Q	R	S	T	U/VW	X	Y	Z
A	a	b	c	d	e	f	g	h	ij	k	l	m	n	o	p	q	r	s	t	u/vw	x	y	z
B	b	c	d	e	f	g	h	ij	k	l	m	n	o	p	q	r	s	t	u/vw	x	y	z	a
C	c	d	e	f	g	h	ij	k	l	m	n	o	p	q	r	s	t	u/vw	x	y	z	a	b
D	d	e	f	g	h	ij	k	l	m	n	o	p	q	r	s	t	u/vw	x	y	z	a	b	c
E	e	f	g	h	ij	k	l	m	n	o	p	q	r	s	t	u/vw	x	y	z	a	b	c	d
F	f	g	h	ij	k	l	m	n	o	p	q	r	s	t	u/vw	x	y	z	a	b	c	d	e
G	g	h	ij	k	l	m	n	o	p	q	r	s	t	u/vw	x	y	z	a	b	c	d	e	f
H	h	ij	k	l	m	n	o	p	q	r	s	t	u/vw	x	y	z	a	b	c	d	e	f	g
J	ij	k	l	m	n	o	p	q	r	s	t	u/vw	x	y	z	a	b	c	d	e	f	g	h
K	k	l	m	n	o	p	q	r	s	t	u/vw	x	y	z	a	b	c	d	e	f	g	h	ij
L	l	m	n	o	p	q	r	s	t	u/vw	x	y	z	a	b	c	d	e	f	g	h	ij	k
M	m	n	o	p	q	r	s	t	u/vw	x	y	z	a	b	c	d	e	f	g	h	ij	k	l
N	n	o	p	q	r	s	t	u/vw	x	y	z	a	b	c	d	e	f	g	h	ij	k	l	m
O	o	p	q	r	s	t	u/vw	x	y	z	a	b	c	d	e	f	g	h	ij	k	l	m	n
P	p	q	r	s	t	u/vw	x	y	z	a	b	c	d	e	f	g	h	ij	k	l	m	n	o
Q	q	r	s	t	u/vw	x	y	z	a	b	c	d	e	f	g	h	ij	k	l	m	n	o	p
R	r	s	t	u/vw	x	y	z	a	b	c	d	e	f	g	h	ij	k	l	m	n	o	p	q
S	s	t	u/vw	x	y	z	a	b	c	d	e	f	g	h	ij	k	l	m	n	o	p	q	r
T	t	u/vw	x	y	z	a	b	c	d	e	f	g	h	ij	k	l	m	n	o	p	q	r	s
U/VW	u/vw	x	y	z	a	b	c	d	e	f	g	h	ij	k	l	m	n	o	p	q	r	s	t
X	x	y	z	a	b	c	d	e	f	g	h	ij	k	l	m	n	o	p	q	r	s	t	u/vw
Y	y	z	a	b	c	d	e	f	g	h	ij	k	l	m	n	o	p	q	r	s	t	u/vw	x
Z	z	a	b	c	d	e	f	g	h	ij	k	l	m	n	o	p	q	r	s	t	u/vw	x	y
	A	B	C	D	E	F	G	H	IJ	K	L	M	N	O	P	Q	R	S	T	U/VW	X	Y	Z

Vigénère Code

He was devoted to the study of the occult sciences and cabbalism and wrote a number of books on various subjects, amongst others, *Systema integrum Cryptographiae*, in which

c

he dealt with codes and ciphers, borrowing mostly from the Abbot Tritheim; but he was the first to make mention of a vowel cipher, which is not without its merits.

A–b	A–h	A–p
E–c	E–k	E–q
I–d	I–l	I–r
O–f	O–m	O–s
U–g	U–n	U–t

The idea is that if there are two or three 'e's' for instance in a word, the C, K, and Q shall be used one after another, and so for all vowels, while the consonants are first replaced by corresponding vowels in the cipher, thus:

EMPEROR OF AUSTRIA would be:
c o a k i f i   fo   bgouidh

This could be further improved by placing dummy letters between words and writing them either in groups of five or continuously, the idea being to prevent deciphering by means of a frequency table, which starts with vowels. The duke also mentioned an invented alphabet attributed traditionally to Solomon. Here it is:

Solomon's Alphabet

The name of Francis Bacon has in recent times been associated with the subject of codes and ciphers by reason of the Shakespeare-Bacon controversy; but, apart from this, Bacon—philosopher, scientist, essayist, poet, and Lord Chancellor of England—made his own contribution to the science of codes and ciphers. One of his codes has been already referred to; and here is another:

A	B	C	D	E	F	G	H
aaaaa	aaaab	aaaba	aaabb	aabaa	aabab	aabba	aabbb
I(J)	K	L	M	N	O	P	Q
abaaa	abaab	ababa	ababb	abbaa	abbab	abbba	abbbb
R	S	T	U(V)	W	X	Y	Z
baaaa	baaab	baaba	baabb	babaa	babab	babba	babbb

(From *De Dignitate et Augmentis Scientiarum*, Book VI, Edition 1623.)

When the Shakespeare-Bacon controversy was at its height at the end of the nineteenth century, a Mrs. Gallup, reading this cipher, wondered why Bacon should invent it and use it in the printing of books. Ciphers generally are made to be used at a moment's notice, and he himself says that ciphers should be easy to read and write; but to set up a book in several different types is an expensive process, and nobody would do it without a reason. This reason Mrs. Gallup set to work to find. She carefully studied the first edition of one of Bacon's early works, and on the title-page, hidden under two sets of italics, she discovered the name of William Rowley—Bacon's chief secretary.

She went on with the work of deciphering and wrote several books on the subject. She claimed to have found this cipher not only in the books of Bacon himself but also in the early editions of works by Greene, Marlowe, Shakespeare, and Ben Jonson. But her startling claim was that the enciphered story thus hidden proved that Bacon was the author of all Shakespeare's plays, and, furthermore, that he was the eldest son of Queen Elizabeth by her first marriage to the Earl of Leicester, which took place while she was imprisoned in the Tower by Queen Mary.

In any case, in the first edition of Shakespeare's works, published by Isaac Jaggard in 1623, Mrs. Gallup claims to have found the following message, enciphered in the 'L. Digges' Poem.

'Francis of Verulam is the author of all the plays heretofore published by Marlowe, Greene, Peele and Shakespeare, and of the twenty-two (plays) now put out for the first time. Some are altered to continue his history. Fr. St. A.'

The difference between the two sets of italic founts being very small, it is an extremely difficult matter to decipher these messages. But for us the important point is that cipher was employed as a weapon in this controversy.

Francis Bacon himself, however, introduced into his charge of treason against the Earl of Somerset the fact that the accused communicated with his friends in cipher, 'a process reserved for Kings and Princes in their affairs of State.'

Another famous trial, where the charges brought against the accused were based on deciphered correspondence, was that of Charles I. It is alleged by some that Charles was beheaded because of the letters he wrote to his wife in cipher, denouncing his enemies and plotting against the Parliament. These papers were captured at the battle of Naseby and were deciphered by a Dr. Wallis.

The beginning of a more scientific approach to the business of codes and ciphers becomes apparent about this time.

It is exemplified in the case of the Spaniards, who wished to maintain close relations between the different parts of their vast and scattered empire. At that time the Spanish dominions included the Netherlands, part of Italy, and all the New World in South America. Naturally enough they desired to keep their internal communications private, and invented for that purpose a special alphabet composed of fifty arbitrary signs. Though this was of the greatest use to them during the League Wars and their constant enmity with France, it was nevertheless not quite as efficient as they had imagined. Henry IV intercepted a few of their dispatches, and asked a well-known professor of geometry—Viette— to see if he could decipher them. The mathematician, acquainted with the 'frequency law', succeeded in finding the key to the secret alphabet in all its variations, and for two years the French Foreign Office deciphered Spanish dispatches, which they seized and afterwards sent on so that the Spaniards would suspect nothing. Eventually, of course, the Spanish government found out what was going on and accused Henry IV, who was a Protestant, of having magicians at his service and of invoking the help of the devil in order to find out Spanish cryptographic secrets, maintaining that he could only have deciphered the messages by calling up the spirits of those who had known the cipher during their earthly life.

But times were changed. Rome was acquainted with the works of Cardan and Porta and the Pope had a sense of humour. He forwarded the complaint to be investigated by a commission of cardinals 'with urgent recommendation'. The cardinals were not slow to understand the Pope's intention, and their investigations into this grave matter are not yet completed.

At the beginning of the eighteenth century the Elector of

Brandenburg—Frederick III—decided that he ought to be crowned king and convert his duchy into the kingdom of Prussia. But without the consent and support of the Emperor —the head of the Holy Roman Empire and titular ruler of all Germany—it was almost impossible to accomplish this. Negotiations were accordingly started with the Court of Vienna, the capital of the Empire, which was not too keen to grant such an exceptional honour to a growing duchy lest it become too powerful, and for years the negotiations languished without any result. The Minister of the duchy at the Viennese Court, Baron Bartholdi, used for his correspondence with Frederick III a figure cipher, in which well-known persons constantly mentioned in dispatches were specially numbered—a common practice.

Amongst these was a Jesuit, Father Wolf, the confessor of the Emperor's Austrian Ambassador in Berlin; he was numbered 116. He played a significant role in the petty diplomatic intrigues of the times, and was a personage of some importance. Frederick III was number 24 and the Emperor number 110.

One day Bartholdi sent a message from Vienna saying that 24 (the Elector Frederick) should write a personal letter in his own handwriting to 110 (the Emperor); but the letter was hastily written, and the 'o' of 110 was taken for 6, reading 116 = Father Wolf.

Frederick did not hesitate, and wrote in his own hand a letter to Father Wolf, stating his reasons for wishing to convert the duchy into a kingdom, and requesting the Jesuit to help him accomplish his project.

Father Wolf was as surprised as he was flattered to receive such an important communication. He decided to do all he could through the powerful order of Jesuits to help a prince who requested the help of the church in the furtherance of

FROM THE MIDDLE AGES ONWARDS 39

his plans. He wrote a letter to the Father Confessor of the Emperor, and he communicated with the General of the Society of Jesus in Rome; the church decided in favour of the Elector; pressure was brought to bear on the Emperor, and, thanks to the original misreading of the cipher, Frederick quickly obtained the consent of the Austrian Court and was crowned King of Prussia.

History does not relate what form the gratitude of Frederick took to the poor Jesuit Father who really got him his crown, but one hopes that he was suitably rewarded.

History has many other celebrated names of men who used cipher, among them Cardinal Richelieu in France.

The Duc de Broglie mentions in his book, *The King's Secret*, a jargon cipher—a kind of dictionary code—which Richelieu used in his private correspondence. A similar one was employed also by Mazarin. In this jargon 'Coxcomb' stood for Grand Duke, 'Garden' for Rome, 'Rose' for the Pope, 'Greyhound' for the Emperor, 'May Lily' for Cardinal de Medici, 'Cornice' for the Queen. At that time the substitution of the names of flowers for the names of real people was quite common. Richelieu himself gave such a code in his own journal.

But for his state correspondence with Louis XIV he occasionally used a very clever form of transposition cipher with a multiple key. Here is an example:

Key : 2741635 ; 15243 ; 671852493 ; 0728615943
Plain text : LETTER SENT TO THE
Key :   2 7 4 1 6 3 5 1 5 2 4 3 6 7 1
Plain text : EMPEROR GIVING FULL
Key :   8 5 2 4 9 3 0 7 2 8 6 1 5 9 4 3 2
Plain text : DETAILS
Key :   7 4 1 6 3 5 1

	1st keyword	2nd keyword	3rd keyword
	1 2 3 4 5 6 7	1 2 3 4 5	1 2 3 4 5 6 7 8 9
Cipher:	TLRTSEE	ETOTN	EPOEMTHER

	4th keyword	1st keyword again
	1 2 3 4 5 6 7 8 9 0	1 2 3 4 5 6 7
Cipher:	NILUGIGVFR	TLIESAD, etc.

Cryptogram: TLRTSEE ETOTN EPOEMTHER NILUGIGVFR TLIESAD, etc.

Louis XIV used a code in communicating with his ambassadors abroad of so complicated a nature that it was not until 175 years after his death that it was deciphered. Louis had several officers and ministers who were very useful to him in this respect. Bazeries, an able French officer interested in cryptography, and author of three interesting books on the subject, who in 1891 deciphered the cryptograms of Louis XIV, found six hundred numbers in the *grand chiffre*. Some were letters and some were syllables. For example, the one word 'mine' could be written in four different ways:

I.	46	144		III.	514	184	374
II.	230	59	125	IV.	535	229	146

It was during the reign of Louis XIV that passports were first used. The French Foreign Minister, the Count de Vergennes, invented them, and they were disguised as letters of introduction, without which people seldom travelled in those days. Thus, with the aid of his ambassadors abroad, Vergennes was kept supplied with exact information about people travelling in France without the travellers themselves being aware of it. Their country of origin was shown by the colour of the card; green was used for Holland, white for Portugal, yellow for England, red for Spain, white and yellow for Venice, red and green for Switzerland, green and yellow for Sweden, green and white for Russia, red and white for the Holy Roman Empire, and so on.

The age of the bearer was shown by the form of the card; if it was circular, he was under twenty-five; oval, between twenty-five and thirty; octagonal, between thirty and forty-five, etc.

Lines placed under the name of the bearer showed his height. If he was tall and thin the lines were parallel and wavy; if he was tall and fat they touched together in the middle; shortness was shown by short strokes, and so on. Even the expression of the face was shown by placing, purely as an ornament, a flower on the border of the card—a rose meant an open frank and friendly person; a tulip a distinguished and pensive one, etc.

A ribbon round the top of the card showed by its length whether the bearer was married, single, or widowed. Another ornamental scroll round the border showed whether he was rich or poor. If he was Catholic a point was was placed behind his name, if he was Protestant a comma, if he was Lutheran a semicolon, Jew a dash, etc. Curiously enough an atheist was left without any sign.

Using more ornamentation, so common in those days, such signs as:

supplied various other information about the traveller, and the Minister, being sent the 'Passe Porte' (to pass the ports of embarkation), knew at once who he was, whether a person of consequence or not; gambler, crook, or duellist; doctor, journalist, or author; a reliable person or one who might be suspected of evil designs; while all that was ostensibly stated on the card was that 'M. Alber Van der Domn is recommended to the Count of Vergennes by M. de Oudenarde, French Ambassador at Naples'.

In those days the financial side of this work was very remunerative. Louvois, French minister of war, is reputed to have paid £120 to a certain Vimbois for discovering a cipher, and four days later paid the same sum to Sieur de la Tixère for a discovery of the same kind.

The Man in the Iron Mask

We now come to a state secret around which, for the last two hundred years, many authors and poets have allowed their imagination to play. It is the story of the 'Man in the Iron Mask', the mystery of which was not solved until 1893, when Bazeries deciphered the coded letter of Louvois which committed the man to prison.

The following are the facts that were generally known about the Man in the Iron Mask. He was imprisoned in the Bastille, in Pignerole, and a third prison in the south of France; he was treated with great respect by all the prison governors, with whom he usually took his meals; he habitually addressed them in the second person singular, as one would in French address persons of inferior rank. He was always exceedingly well dressed and was waited upon with great deference. One day he scratched something on a silver plate and threw it out of a window; it was picked up by a yokel, who, hoping for a good tip, took it straight to the prison authorities. To his dismay he was immediately flung into prison himself, where he stayed for several months, and was not released until all his antecedents were investigated by the police, and it was learned that he did not know how to read or write.

In the French archives was found a copy of a letter, written in *grand chiffre*, addressed to Catinat, Commander-in-Chief of French Forces, and the following is the translation of this letter as deciphered by Bazeries:

> It is not necessary to explain to you in detail how ill-pleased is His Majesty having learned that against your orders M. de Bulonde has raised the siege of Coni and that he retreated even in a disorderly fashion. H.M. knows very well the consequences of such disaster and the prejudice with which the news will be received that this fortress was not taken, and that we shall have to repeat this operation during the winter.
>
> H.M. desires that you arrest M. de Bulonde and accompany him to the Citadel of Pignerole where H.M. wishes him to be incarcerated during the night, being allowed to walk on the ramparts during the day but wearing an iron mask.
>
> As the Governor of Pignerole is under your orders will you send him the necessary authority for execution.
>
> (*Signed*) LOUVOIS.

It was none other than Vivien Labbé, Seigneur de Bulonde, Knight of the Military Order of St. Louis, Governor of Dinan, Grand Master of the Orders of Notre Dame de Carmel and St. Lazare of Jerusalem, Lieutenant-General of the Royal Forces. Needless to say, Bazeries had his cipher key checked by other papers which all confirmed that it was correct.

This cipher is similar to one used by Napoleon, and it is evident, therefore, that for over a hundred years the French governments used ciphers based on exactly the same principles. Apart from the *grand chiffre*, another one called the *petit chiffre* was used for all communications between the armies and the General Staff. Here is an example of the *petit chiffre*:

44   CODES AND CIPHERS

Napoleon's (Petit Chiffre) Cipher
Reconstructed by Bazeries

A–15, ar–25, al–39
B–37, bu–3, bo–35, bi–29
C–6, ca–32, ce–20
D–23, de–52
E–53, es–82, et–50, en–68
F–55, fa–69, fe–58, fo–71
G–81, ga–51
H–85, hi–77
I–119, is–122
J–87, jai–123
K– ?
L–96, lu–103, le–117, la–106
M–114, ma–107
N–115, ne–94, ni–116
O–90, ot–153
P–137, po–152
Q–173, que–136
R–169, ra–146, re–126, ri–148
S–167, sa–171, se–177, si–134, so–168, su–174
T–176, ti–145, to–157
U–138
V–164, ve–132, vi–161, vo–175
W, X, Y– ?
Z–166

Louis XIV and Louis XV used a very similar cipher, based on exactly the same principles, which were probably laid down by M. Vimbois and Sieur de la Tixère, commissioned by Louvois.

The French Revolution

Napoleon owed his *grand chiffre*, which was used only for secret correspondence between himself and his generals, to a member of the revolutionary tribunal and one of his enemies during his consulship, who wrote a treatise on ciphers which is not of great interest to-day. But what is interesting is that Napoleon was the first to treat army ciphers seriously.

General Suchet had his ciphers stolen by the Spaniards, who used them to facilitate the recapture of Mequina and Lerida.

General Bardin attributes the débâcle of 1814 to the fact that, during the retreat from Russia, the French army lost practically all its cipher officers, and when Napoleon wanted to write to the garrisons stationed abroad and the forces scattered about in France, Berthier, his chief of Staff, had to communicate his orders in plain language, with the unfortunate result that few of these dispatches arrived at their destination and many fell into the hands of the enemy. 'Perhaps,' says Bardin, 'the future of France and the map of Europe depended then on the use of cryptography.'

Nevertheless, as late as 1870 the French army used such a poor cipher that when one of the French military attachés sent a dispatch to the War Minister and it could not be deciphered because the chief of the department was absent, the minister asked one of the officers to try to break the cipher without the key. In a very few hours his own son, Captain Berthaut, managed to do so.

The German army has always been very efficient in the use of cyphers, the officers being taught a special course of cryptography, and Max Hernig, in his history of the siege of Paris in 1871, states that it was because the besieged communicated with the French army in the provinces in a very elementary cipher that the Germans were victorious.

At the end of the nineteenth century the Russian Nihilists used a double cipher, which, having been transposed vertically, was then transposed horizontally; but they made the mistake of using the same keyword in both transpositions. As it is a common variation of double columnar cipher, we give it as an example:

$$\frac{\textit{Keyword:}\quad\quad\quad\quad\quad\text{SCHUVALOF}}{\textit{Alphabetical sequence of letters:}\ \ 6\ 2\ 3\ 7\ 8\ 1\ 4\ 5\ 9} = \frac{\text{ACHLOSUVF}}{1\ 2\ 3\ 4\ 5\ 6\ 7\ 8\ 9}$$

Now suppose we have to encipher the following: 'Reunion to-morrow at three p.m. Bring arms as we shall attempt to bomb the railway station. Chief.'

CODES AND CIPHERS

	1	2	3	4	5	6	7	8	9
1	R	E	U	N	I	O	N	T	O
2	M	O	R	R	O	W	A	T	T
3	H	R	E	E	P	M	B	R	I
4	N	G	A	R	M	S	A	S	W
5	E	S	H	A	L	L	A	T	T
6	E	M	P	T	T	O	B	O	M
7	B	T	H	E	R	A	I	L	W
8	A	Y	S	T	A	T	I	O	N
9	C	H	I	E	F	A	B	C	D

The 'abcd' at the end are 'nulls' used to fill in the squares.

Now we transpose the message according to the letter sequence of the keyword:

	6	2	3	7	8	1	4	5	9
6	O	M	P	B	O	E	T	T	M
2	W	O	R	A	T	M	R	O	T
3	M	R	E	B	R	H	E	P	I
7	A	T	H	I	L	B	E	R	W
8	T	Y	S	I	O	A	T	A	N
1	O	E	U	N	T	R	N	I	O
4	S	G	A	A	S	N	R	M	W
5	L	S	H	A	T	E	A	L	T
9	A	H	I	B	C	C	E	F	D

So the message reads:

OMPBOETTMWORATMROTMREBRHEPIATHILBE
RWTYSIOATANOEUNTRNIOSGAASNRMWLSHAT
EALTAHIBCCEFD

In all languages where certain letters must follow or precede certain others, the deciphering of this script will never present difficulties. We first count the number of letters in the script (81), which will give the size of the square (9×9), and once this is done all we have to do is to remember that in nine cases out of ten 'h' follows either 't' or 's' or 'c', and that the bigrams such as AT, TO, WE, and the very helpful (English) trigram 'the', and the doubles TT, LL, EE, etc., are the most common. In fact, the Russian police soon found out all about that conspiracy.

In modern times cryptography is made full use of quite scientifically and methodically. At the beginning of the war of 1914-18 a professor of mathematics was invited by the Admiralty to organize a special deciphering department known as Room 40. OB, and it was due to the brilliant team work of that department that a German telegram, sending instructions to the German Ambassador in Mexico to organize active intervention in return for territorial concessions from U.S.A., was decoded. That telegram played a very important part in bringing the United States on to the side of the Allies.

One of the later triumphs of deciphering was during the Naval Disarmament Conference. Japanese experts used a cipher, with several transpositions, based on an extinct Manchurian dialect of the fifteenth century. This was 'broken'—i.e., deciphered—by the Foreign Office cryptographic bureau in forty-eight hours.

CHAPTER III

SIGNALS, SIGNS, AND SECRET LANGUAGES

BEFORE we go to the more complicated codes of to-day, let us examine a method of signalling which, in different forms, has been in use since the first hollowed tree-trunk was launched on the sea.

The first actual records of signals at sea are mentioned in Greek mythology when Aegeus sent his son to Crete and agreed with him beforehand that a white flag should be displayed if he reached it safely. Virgil also mentions that Agamemnon signalled from his ship to Sinon in the citadel —but these were probably not signals as we understand them. Certain flags, torches, or a sound may have conveyed an agreed meaning, but not letters or words. We have already mentioned Polybius' system of torch signals in the historical survey in the first chapter; this was the first signalling code ever invented, but we must note also in this connexion a code of Joachimus Fortius whereby three torches were used in this manner:

One torch alone=first 8 letters of the alphabet—ABCDEFGH.
Two torches together=next 8 letters of the alphabet—IKLMNOPQ.
Three torches together=the rest of the alphabet—RSTVWXYZ.

and to differentiate between these three groups—one light used once stood for the letter 'A', one light twice for 'B', two lights for 'I', two lights twice for 'K', and so on.

SIGNALS, SIGNS, AND SECRET LANGUAGES 49

Before the advent of wireless, ships at sea relied very much more than they do now on their visual signals. This is the numerical code of light signals which is still used very frequently, with four lights only, placed on the foremast.

```
O   = 1         O
                O
O               |  = 7
O   = 2         O
O               O

O
O   = 3         O
O               |
                O  = 8      These lights should be placed at
O               O           least fifteen or twenty feet apart;
O               O           and for 5, 6, etc., the highest light
O   = 4                     should be hoisted at the masthead
O                           and the lowest one at the ensign
                O           staff.
O               O
|               O  = 9
O   = 5         |
O               O

                A false fire = 10.
O
O
|   = 6
O
```

During the days of sailing-ships signalling lights were used placed on the cross made by the mast and spars, i.e., vertically and horizontally to each other. But now this has been superseded by the Morse code, the flashes of which are made by powerful electrical projectors.

D

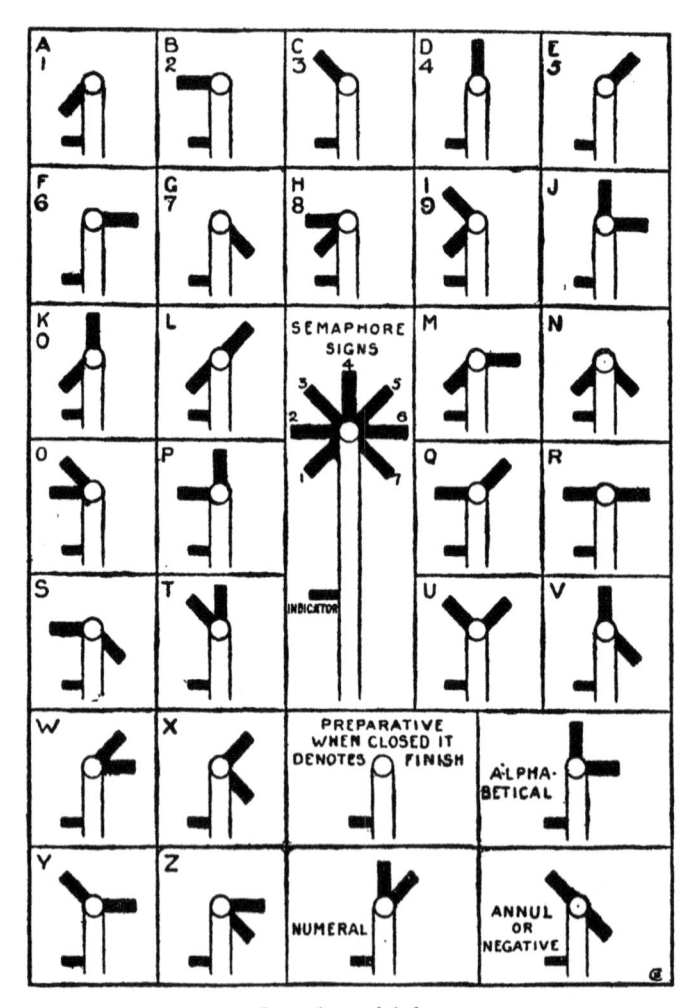

Semaphore alphabet

SIGNALS, SIGNS, AND SECRET LANGUAGES 51

Semaphore, however, is still in use, and most people are familiar with this form of signalling, which is done either with flags or signal arms. The arms move in a circle which is divided into eight parts, each of 45 degrees; seven of the parts are the letters A—G, and the eighth position is where the arms are placed when not in use.

Procedure Signals and Special Signs

General Answer	A	Separating whole number	
Who are you	R̄Ū	from fractions	M̄M̄
Full stop	ĀĀĀ	Move lower (or closer)	MO
End of message	AR	Move to your right	MR
You are correct	C	Wait	Q
Hyphen	D̄Ū	Message received	R
Horizontal bar	ĒX̄	Inverted commas	R̄R̄
Decimal point	FI	Block capitals	ŪK̄
Closing down	GB	I have nothing to commu-	
Number of words	GR	nicate at present	V̄Ā
Break sign	II	Calling up sign. Sent con-	
Repeat signal	IMI	tinuously until answered.	
Carry on	K	Alphabetical call sign or	,
Brackets	K̄K̄	letter	J
Move higher (or farther)	MH	Word after	WA
Move to your left	ML	Word before	WB
		Oblique stroke	X̄Ē

Heraldry

The fact that heraldry should come into a book dealing with codes and ciphers may seem a little strange, but is not heraldry an abbreviated and, to most people, a secret way of giving a person's family antecedents? It is a more beautiful and picturesque form of the laundry mark.

It may also sound rather strange to say that the use of flags had its origin in the belief in the transmigration of souls; nevertheless, this appears to be true. Certain tribes of semi-savage people believed that when they died their souls would live again in the form of an animal (primitive totemism), and to be sure that they returned into that of a worthy animal, they often wore amulets, made out of rough pottery or clay, about their person during their lifetime. The stories of the werewolf remind us of this old belief, and the practice of wearing lucky charms and carrying mascots on motor-cars may be regarded as a survival of it.

It is not surprising that whole tribes of people gradually took for their emblem the same animal—after all, if you are going to heaven, you prefer to go to the same heaven as your friends and relations are going to—and so it came about that the lion or the leopard became the sign or emblem of a whole tribe. This was the beginning of heraldry. The people of strong fighting instincts quite naturally would take a fighting animal for their souls to continue in after death, while the peace-lovers might take a dove.

Heraldry did not reach England until the time of Henry II and Richard Cœur de Lion. In those days armorial bearings were of real practical use: since the knights were encased entirely in armour, the only way of recognizing them was by their insignia—both figures and colours.

The last de Clare owed his death on the field of Bannockburn to his having neglected to wear his coat of arms; had he been recognized his great value as a prisoner would have saved him. Also the loss of the battle of Barnet was in part attributed to the similarity between the royal cognizance of the sun and that of John de Vere, Earl of Oxford—a star with streamers—Warwick charging Oxford in mistake for the King.

This shows how very important it was to have your coat

SIGNALS, SIGNS, AND SECRET LANGUAGES 53

of arms legibly drawn and coloured. At first it was only the nobles who had heraldic designs, but gradually they allowed their vassals to wear their colours, in much the same way as the members of a football team all wear shirts of the same colour.

A grant of arms at the hand of a sovereign also had a great value. The glories of heraldry reached their zenith in the reign of Richard II, but it was not until the reign of Richard III that it was thought necessary to place the whole heraldry of the kingdom under control.

There is a story of later times about John Gibbon, the heraldic author, having a quarrel with two maiden ladies of the same name. He obtained a licence to convert the scallops in their armorial coat into the black balls called 'ogresses', a most heraldic revenge!

To-day, states, cities, corporations, business houses, and colleges have their arms; there are family or paternal arms, and arms of alliance which are granted when members of two families are united in marriage.

The first known transformation of a private coat of arms into a national flag took place in recent times when the paternal coat of the Washington family became the Stars and Stripes of the United States (*argent*, 2 bars *gules*, in chief 3 mullets of the second). The terms for describing a flag are the same as those applied in heraldry to the corresponding parts of a shield. Banners, standards, and ensigns are mentioned in the Bible, and in the time of Marius, the *Vexillum* was used. This was a square piece of cloth fastened to a length of wood fixed crosswise to the end of a spear. But drapery was not used for flags until the Middle Ages. Before that the Persians, for example, fixed an eagle to the end of a lance, and also represented the sun, as their divinity, upon their standards, which appear to have been formed of some kind of textile, and were guarded by the bravest men in the army.

In Greece a purple dress placed on the end of a spear was a signal to advance, and the North American Indians carried poles fledged with feathers from the wings of eagles.

The question of the *insignia militaria* of the Romans is a very important one, having direct bearing on the history of heraldry and on the origin of national, family, and personal devices. It was by them that the custom was reduced to a system.

In the British army the standards of the cavalry are the same colour as the regimental facings; they bear the insignia, cipher, number, and honours of the regiment and are richly ornamented.

In the Navy the white flag with St. George's cross is borne by Admirals, Vice-Admirals, and Rear-Admirals on their flagships. All ships in the Navy fly the White Ensign; the Blue Ensign is borne by ships in the service of various public offices, and also, under certain restrictions, by such ships as are commanded by officers of the Naval Reserve. The Red Ensign is borne by all ships of the Merchant Navy.

Yacht clubs are given certain privileges. The Royal Yacht Squadron is allowed to fly the White Ensign, and others to carry the Blue Ensign with characteristic burgees.

Signals

A system of naval signals comprises different methods of conveying orders or information from one ship to another within sight and hearing, but at a distance too great to permit of hailing—in other words, beyond the reach of the voice even when aided by the speaking-trumpet.

Of course, now that wireless is so widely used, flags are not needed so much, although the disadvantage of wireless is that the enemy can pick up any message, and will only have to decode it. And not only will your message be understood, but the recipient can discover where it comes from. For these reasons, whenever possible, the Navy still uses the older method of signalling.

Signals are divided into classes according to the instruments by which they are made. There are sight and sound signals; flag, semaphore, fixed and flashing lamps, fireworks, horn or steam-whistle, and gun signals; day, night, fog, and distant signals. Besides these, there are other divisions, such as general, vocabulary, evolutionary, etc., which depend upon technical considerations and are matters of arrangement.

Flag Code

Towards 1780 Admiral Kempenfelt devised a plan of flag-signalling which was the parent of that now in use. There are two sets of flags—one of ten numbered from 1 to 10, and another of twenty-one called after the letters of the alphabet. There are also pennants and a few special flags. The number flags are used with the general signal book, a kind of dictionary in which figures stand opposite sentences conveying orders or announcements. Opposite 123 might stand 'hoist all boats'. The letter flags are used with the vocabulary signal book, in which, opposite collections of letters, are put single words or small groups of words. Thus, ABC might represent the word 'Admiral', and STO the phrase 'will sail at noon'. The general code is used for words of command, and the vocabulary for long communications.

The night signal book contains a limited number of definite orders and announcements, made known by exhibiting lanterns, never more than four, arranged vertically, horizontally, or in a square. For a few signals some kind of firework is displayed. Fog-signals are made by firing different numbers of guns at fixed intervals. But owing to the slowness of flag-code signalling it has been largely superseded by semaphore. Distant signals, now rarely used, are made by hoisting flags of different shapes at distances at which colours become invisible.

At sea the striking of the flag denotes surrender, and the flag of one country being placed over that of another denotes the victory of the former. A yellow flag denotes infectious disease and quarantine, and the universally understood flag of truce is white.

The Bush Telegraph in Africa

When you do not understand something it often appears to be magic. The African natives on hearing a gramophone for the first time have thought it was a god or a devil; and in the same way, many a European has been completely mystified by the way in which the natives got to know of certain facts three or four days before they themselves knew about them. They may have thought it telepathy, but in the majority of cases the explanation is simply the drum.

I spent several years in the African bush and I was determined to learn the secret of this native method of communication. I found that it was a large drum hollowed out of a solid tree with a longitudinal opening, the edges carved to form two parallel 'lips', one considerably thinner than the other. One is called the male and the other the female, and by striking one after the other, low and high sounds are produced almost as dots and dashes of the Morse code. I heard these throbbing noises after nightfall in Africa and, talking by camp fires with the local village elders, found that the 'language' of the tom-toms is a well-organized code handed down from generation to generation within certain families.

It is composed not only of high and low sounds, but also of short and long sounds. The drum, being hollow, vibrates with a booming noise when struck, and this can be stopped by placing a hand against the opening in the same way as you stop a glass from vibrating by touching it.

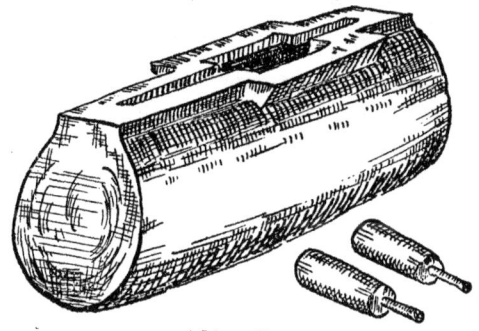

African Drum

I give an example—the word is NKOY, which is my native name and was the first word I learnt on the drum.

O = long sound, I = short sound.

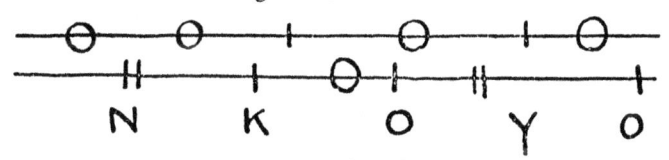

Language of the drums

The families who know this code also know how to make the drum—actually it is not a drum at all, as there is no skin stretched over a round opening. Making the drum is a very complicated operation, especially in view of the primitive tools with which the delicate work of hollowing the wooden cylinder, through a very narrow top, has to be carried out; and, after it is roughly shaped, the even more delicate carving of the thickness of the two sides must be made so as to produce the two distinct high- and low-pitched sounds.

When ready it is mounted on an ant-hill (the ant-hills in Africa are made of hard clay and are as high as a room) and a hole is dug right through the middle, to convey the sound through the earth. Whenever possible the spot is situated near a river, as water carries sound very well. Often a few palm leaves are placed over the drum to protect it from the rain. After a suitable 'christening' ceremony, when a goat is sacrificed and the new drum is given a drink of arak or palm wine, an appropriate name is found for it and it starts to 'speak'. The natives eagerly listen to the answer from other drums whose range is known. The average range of a small drum is from six to ten miles; bigger ones have a range of well over twenty miles. One which I had made for myself had a constant reliable range of twenty-two miles along the river, while with a suitable wind and in moist air (moist air after rain is a good sound conductor) the range was found to be almost forty miles.

Now in the villages the 'drum family', hearing a drum being beaten and calling them, would answer on their own drum near their hut, and thus transmit the message along farther and farther, by relays. Everything can be said on the drum: news of a large steamer coming up the river, of a white man desiring food for his porters from the next village, of a government official calling up certain tribes to pay head-taxes, and so on.

When I asked the natives why the drum was beaten and what it was saying, they would call up the local 'drum man', and he would translate the sound into a kind of sing-song, using certain set phrases and often words not found in the native vocabulary. When questioned he would say that it was a 'drum-word' meaning so-and-so.

This shows that the drum code is almost a dictionary code, and I have an idea that it is based on vowels forming the four possible sound combinations into set words, of which there can be a maximum of a hundred and twenty.

SIGNALS, SIGNS, AND SECRET LANGUAGES

Tramps' Code

Another method of making signals, and one which, like the tom-tom, is used by one set of people only, is the Tramps' Code. It is widely known that tramps have their own method of communicating with each other, and that

- = nothing doing, disagreeable people.
- = danger.
- = beware of prison.
- = nothing here.
- = food may be had for the asking (hot cross bun?)
- = the tramp may get what he wants by threatening the occupants.
- = people of authority live here.
- = very bad. They give you in charge here.
- = householder may yield to eloquence (the open mouth?)
- = jagged teeth means beware of the dog.
- = a warning that the owner of the house is liable to use force.
- = three small circles represent coins. The owner of the house may give money.
- = too many tramps have been here already.
- = no good.
- = bad people, offer work.
- = spearhead pointing downward urges the tramp to take vengeance for his predecessor, as he was given a rough time. In some cases this means that he was offered work in exchange for food.

Tramps' Signs

the chalk marks which are frequently seen on house doors and walls are indications from one wanderer to another.

The code is kept very secret, and it was only by mere chance that the French police managed to get the foregoing list. It was found in the pocket of a tramp who was arrested, scribbled on some soiled paper. He was evidently a novice, for on inquiry it was found that the code is handed down from generation to generation, and no tramp born in the profession would need to carry a written vocabulary.

There are many other signs, such as two-pronged forks, reaping hooks, and geometrical patterns, which all have a meaning of their own, but these are sufficient to enable the householder to look at the wall of his house after a tramp has left him and see what the tramp thinks of him.

Marked Cards

Another system of signalling which is neither code nor cipher in the strict sense, but which nevertheless conveys a meaning to the initiated, is the marked pack of cards. The aspiring conjurer will be interested to know that some of the seemingly miraculous card tricks are not always brought about by sleight of hand. There are packs of cards to be bought in America—and probably by now in England, too—which have their suits and numbers marked on the back as well as on their face. These are so cleverly marked

SIGNALS, SIGNS, AND SECRET LANGUAGES 61

that it would need a very great deal of practice before any one could use them successfully.

The back of the playing-card shown above looks quite normal. Now this card is the nine of hearts. If you look very carefully in the left-hand corner you will find this:

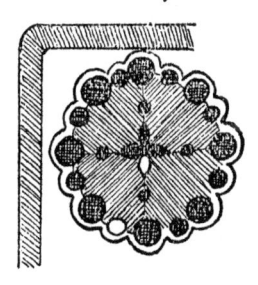

The dots round the edge of the circle are the twelve numbers, plus four 'nulls' put in to make it less obvious. From ace to king (counting in a clockwise direction), you will notice that the ninth is left white. In the inner circle the four leaves signify the suits. The top one is diamonds, to the right clubs, at the bottom hearts, and to the left spades. This is how we realize from the back that this card is the nine of hearts.

Another way of sending messages by cards needs much more preparation as well as certain invisible inks. This method was used a hundred years ago with piquet cards (32 cards). Two people had previously agreed upon the arrangement of cards as regards value and suit. The value could be fixed by a doggerel rhyme, such as

'King Henry the 8th was a Knave to his Queen.'
King   8   Knave   Queen.
'He's one short of seven and nine or ten scenes.'
ace   7   9   10

Or the suits could be arranged in alphabetical order, club, diamond, heart, and spade. You then arrange the cards in order according to the doggerel rhyme—if you were using that—and with your invisible ink write the message, Chinese way, on the backs of the cards. Write down the first column of cards and then the second and so on, not along the top row. This done, shuffle the cards and send them off to their destination.

And then there are the Tic-Tac men, who may be seen at any race meeting, standing on high stools above the crowd gesticulating to each other. They use a form of code. Their secrets are very well kept, but it has been ascertained that they are keeping the levels of the prices among each other. And in this way they do it quickly, privately, and efficiently. On a noisy race-course they could not possibly shout their numbers, nor would they have time to go to a stand several yards farther on; so up in their boxes they play their game of dumb crambo—and let any one interested try to discover exactly what they are saying to each other.

The shop code is used very much more than is commonly realized. For instance, how many people have taken particular notice of the laundry-mark sewn or inked into their linen? And yet this little letter or number in your handkerchief tells the laundry your name and address. Could such information be arranged more discreetly and efficiently?

Another code that one often comes up against is that which indicates the prices of goods in drapery stores. You look at the ticket attached to some article of clothing, expecting to learn the price, and what you see is something like W.X.F. 476. This the assistant immediately translates into '10s. 6d., Madam—isn't it a lovely little model?' and you forget your irritation. Such signs tell the shopkeeper what year the goods came into the shop, at what price he bought them, and at what price he is to sell them.

The antique dealer has a code of his own, and his signs are

unusually complicated and strange. M. André Langie tells an amusing story of an antique shop code. Whilst waiting for a friend who was always a little late, but not usually so much as he was on this occasion, M. Langie found that he was near an antique shop, and with pencil and paper he took down the following details:

1.	Bronze table	2. p. p.
2.	Incense burner	mp. p.
3.	Coloured engraving	m. mp. p.
4.	Large mirror	mp. mp. p.
5.	Card table	e. p. p.
6.	Iron dagger	mp. p.
7.	Picture	mr. p.
8.	Engraving	mi. z.
9.	Picture	mi. z.
10.	Tray	mf. z.
11.	Barometer	m. v. p.
12.	Old picture	f. z.
13.	Four engravings	m. mf. z.
14.	Grandfather clock	f. p. p.
15.	Card table	b. r. p.
16.	Cheese dish	f. z.
17.	Flemish painting	l. mp. p.
18.	Trunk	2. r. p.

It needs no experienced decipherer to notice at once the large number of 'p's'; M. Langie added them up and found that nearly a third of all the letters noted were 'p's' and were among the pence and shilling signs. Also that the letter 'p' was never at the left, but often on the right. And remembering the strange behaviour of zero—how in itself it means nothing, and on the left of another figure retains its symbolism, but put on to the right of any figure it will multiply its value by ten—he decided that the 'p' stood for nought. Then he found that the only other letter in the pence column besides 'p' was 'z'. This he hazarded would stand for 6d.

Then he turned his attention to the shillings column and decided that the letter 'm' stood for 1. He reasoned out that nine is a number rarely found in the price of antiques. An article is more likely to be 10s. or 20s. than 9s. or 19s.; so he decided that 9 was not shown at all.

He then decided that he had deciphered the numbers 0, 1, and 6. He tested this out and found:

2.	Incense Burner	.	.	. 10s.
3.	Coloured engraving .	.	£1 10s.
4.	Large mirror .	.	. £10. 10s. 0d.
6.	Iron Dagger .	.	.	. 10s.

Then he used a little common sense and found that the card table looked as if it was worth £3 5s. So he decided that 'b' = 3 and 'r' = 5. This left numbers 4, 7, and 8 to be found out. He saw that the letter 'f' was in the shillings column, and followed by 'z' which was surely 7s. 6d., so he put 7 to 'f' and read:

10.	Tray	.	.	.	17s. 6d.
12.	Old Picture	.	.	7s. 6d.
13.	Four engravings	.	. £1 17s. 6d.
14.	Grandfather clock .	. £7 0s. 0d.
16.	Cheese dish .	.	.	7s. 6d.

I will leave the reader to work out for himself the values of the remaining letters.

SIGNALS, SIGNS, AND SECRET LANGUAGES 65

Braille

At the beginning of the nineteenth century there were twenty-three different known methods for enabling the blind

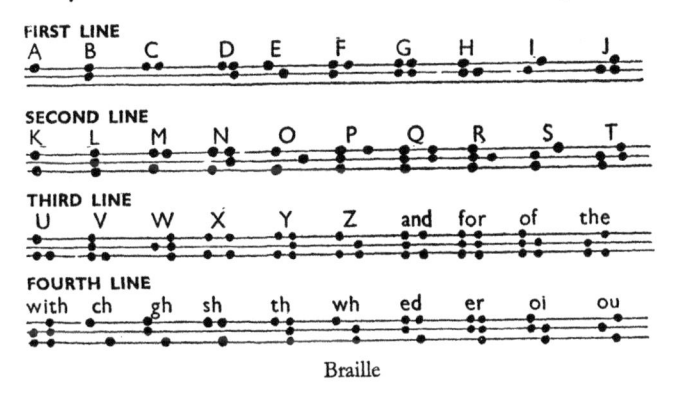

FIRST LINE
A B C D E F G H I J

SECOND LINE
K L M N O P Q R S T

THIRD LINE
U V W X Y Z and for of the

FOURTH LINE
with ch gh sh th wh ed er oi ou

Braille

to read. The very first invention consisted of pins stuck into a cushion in the forms of letters, and it is from this that the Braille system was developed.

Braille himself was a Frenchman who lived from 1809 to 1852; he became blind when three years of age and worked all his life on his invention, but it was not until three years after his death that his system was given official recognition.

His system consists of varying combinations of six dots in an oblong, the vertical side containing three dots and the horizontal two. There are sixty-three combinations of these

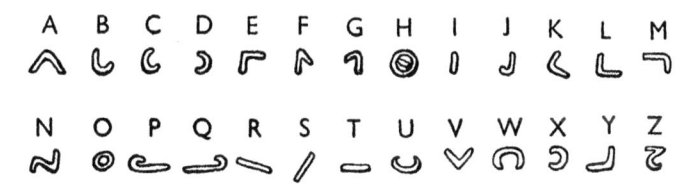

A B C D E F G H I J K L M

N O P Q R S T U V W X Y Z

Dr. Moon's Characters

E

six dots, and after the letters of the alphabet have been provided for, the remaining signs are used for punctuation, contractions, etc.

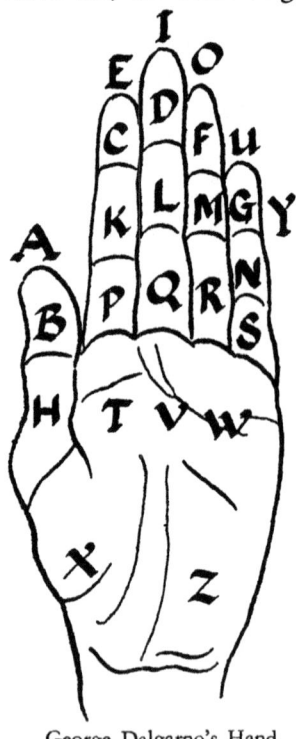

The points are raised and the script is read with the finger tips. There is another alphabet, that of Dr. Moon, which is quite widely known and is based on the Roman letters. But it is Braille's system that is in general use.

Hand Alphabets

It was as early as 700 that John de Beverly taught a deaf mute to speak; but it was not until 1501 that Jerome Cardan proclaimed that the deaf could be taught by writing.

Pedro Ponce and, later, Juan Paulo Bonet, another Spanish monk, started to teach the deaf and dumb to talk with the aid of signs. It was 1648 before John Bulwer wrote the first book on the subject printed in England. It was followed in 1680 by a book by George Dalgarno of Edinburgh, who gave a very concise two-handed alphabet scientifically constructed.

To-day there are two hand alphabets. The one-handed method is used in America, Ireland, and with variations and additions in all European countries. The two-handed method is used in Great Britain and Australia.

George Dalgarno's Hand Alphabet.

SIGNALS, SIGNS, AND SECRET LANGUAGES 67

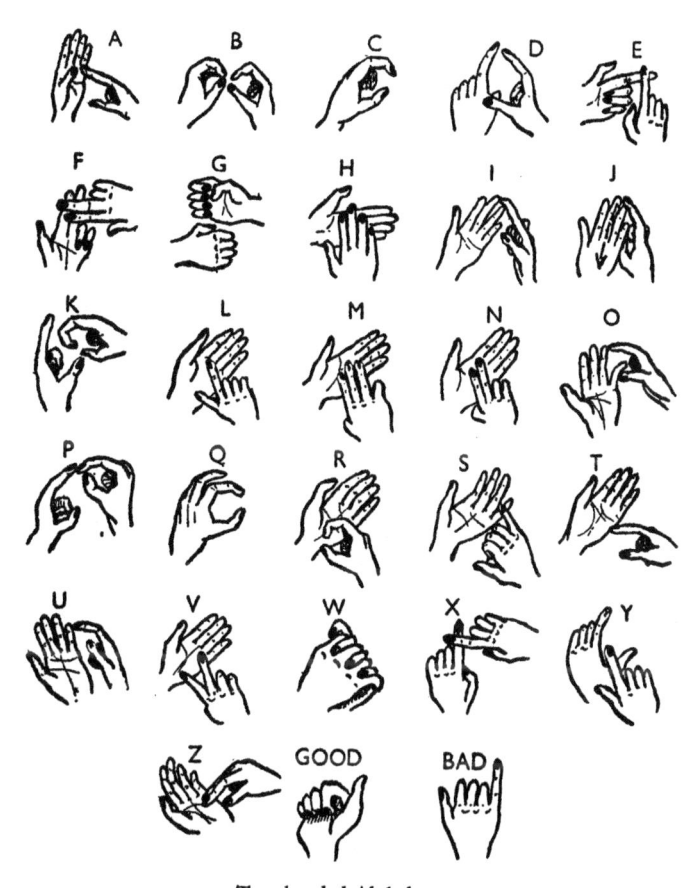

Two-handed Alphabet

Boy Scout Signs

The four principal scout signs derived by Lord Baden-Powell from his experience on the veldt with the Dutch and native scouts before and during the Boer War are as follows:

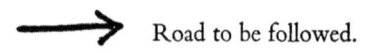

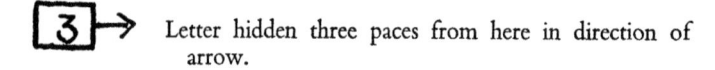

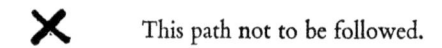

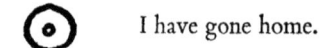

→ Road to be followed.

[3]→ Letter hidden three paces from here in direction of arrow.

✗ This path not to be followed.

⊙ I have gone home.

Boy Scout Signs

Without using any writing the trackers and hunters in the African forest often leave signs for those who follow them. A half-broken twig on a hunter's path indicates that the tracker is in front, while a twig broken off and stuck in the ground in the middle of the path shows that it is the wrong path. Two twigs of two bushes brought together and tied over a path mean beware of wild animals.

A whole branch broken off and placed across the path means danger of elephants. Two twigs broken off and stuck parallel on the edge of a swamp means that the swamp can be crossed; but three twigs crossing each other means swamp impassable.

Different tribes probably have different signs, and the above refer only to the Batua tribes in the Kiwu area in Central Africa, and are given here merely as an example.

Ciphers in Literature

Ciphers in literature have been used by several authors. Balzac in one of his books gave a cryptogram consisting of all the alphabet and signs used ordinarily, and with the letters and signs upside down, in groups of five letters; it is three pages long. A good many people have tried to decipher this, and for a long time nobody could even get an inkling of what it all meant. Finally Bazeries applied scientific methods to the problem, and came to the conclusion that it was merely a leg-pull on the part of the author, and that the solution was hidden in a sentence preceding this hotch-potch of printer's type: 'The question of the Confessor and his lover was an undecipherable (unknown) quantity.'

Edgar Allan Poe in the *Gold Beetle* also uses cryptography, and in Jules Verne's *A Journey to the Centre of the Earth* we see a Danish scholar intent on piecing together the mystery of a parchment that will show him how to get to the interior of the globe. But Professor Lidenbrock seeks too far, and it is Axel, a careless nephew, who deciphers it by reading the finals of the lines backwards.

Yet another well-known author who was evidently conversant with codes and ciphers was Rudyard Kipling. In *The Man Who Would be King*, Carneham refers to 'a string talk letter' used by beggars in the Punjab, and to the cipher made by a knotted twig with a piece of string wound round it.

CHAPTER IV
COMMERCIAL CODES
As has probably been noticed, codes and ciphers are no longer used only by kings and generals, or by clandestine lovers with irate fathers; with growing commercialism there have sprung up codes to help trade.

Lloyd's

In 1688 Edward Lloyd ran a coffee-house in Tower Street, London. He was an enterprising man, and when he found that several brokers used to discuss their business with each other over their coffee, he decided that, to sell still more coffee, he must make things easier for them. So he first instituted a blackboard; and sure enough, still more independent brokers came along and consumed still more coffee while doing their business. Later he brought out a weekly bulletin of shipping information, which was no small undertaking in those days.

In a few years' time Mr. Lloyd gave another example of his enterprise and intelligence by moving his coffee-house to Lombard Street, in the very centre of that portion of the old city of London more frequented by merchants of the highest class. It was not until 1774 that, with the rapid increase of marine insurance business, a committee was set up and a constitution formed which has remained practically unaltered to the present day. Although there is no longer Lloyd's Coffee-house, yet the name is preserved, and 'Lloyd's' is known all over the world as the centre of Marine Insurance business.

One of the first things the members of Lloyd's set themselves to do was to devise some method of signalling between sea and shore, so that advance news of ships and cargoes might be received. A primitive projector was set up; and—contrary to the general notion that large cut-out letters were placed in front of it—a system of light signals based on Polybius' system was started. It was this that probably gave rise later on to the use of codes for commercial purposes; and apart from some invented ciphers used by Venetian merchants in the eighteenth century, the Lloyd's signals were the first to come into use.

The Origin of Commercial Codes

In 1794 a system of rapid communications, then known as aerial telegraphy, employing semaphores on high towers visible at considerable distances, was instituted, and made rapid progress in Europe. Men soon saw that economy as well as secrecy could be achieved by means of codes in which a whole phrase or sentence could be expressed by one group of signals.

In 1825 codes employing figure groups were in common use, and a rather extensive code, called Telegraphic Vocabulary, for the line of semaphore telegraph between Liverpool and Holyhead, was published in London in 1845. In this code there appear words, phrases, and even long sentences, each represented by groups of one to four digits.

In England the earliest practical trial of electric telegraphy was made in 1837 on the London and North Western Railway, and the first public line, under Wheatstone and Coke Patents, was laid from Paddington to Slough on the Great Western Railway in 1843.

In America, in 1860, Brewell published his Mercantile Cipher for condensing telegrams, in which English dictionary words were employed, and in which we find a fairly complete vocabulary, arranged under captions. Such codes, though not in printed form, were already in use amongst the business men in the United States.

The ABC code, also based on dictionary words, first appeared in 1874. Up to 1872 the telegraphic companies, by international agreement, charged pronounceable code language words as plain text; the higher tariff applied only to cipher or numeral language. These were charged for at the rate of five characters per word; and in 1875, at St. Petersburg, the maximum length was fixed for either plain text or code words at seven syllables. This naturally led to abuse, as such words as CHINESISKSLUTNINGSDON—21 letters, but only 6 syllables—were used by coders.

The next telegraphic conference made it plain that this rule applied only to the words of European or Latin origin, not to artificial words. But dictionary words for code use were not very successful, as they led to errors in compiling and reading. Coders had to use invented words, as these avoided not only orthographic errors, but also the possibility of errors in transmission, i.e., the changing of a dot into a dash, etc.

Example : MARROW = NARROW, where M = (Morse) - -, is changed into N = - . ; CITERONS changed to CITRONS, where E = a single dot, was omitted altogether, etc., or for instance misreadings as follows :

$$\begin{array}{cccccc} B & A & N & E & F & U & L \\ -\cdots & \cdot- & -\cdot & \cdot & \cdots- & \cdot\cdot- & \cdot-\cdot\cdot \end{array}$$

into

$$\begin{array}{cccccc} D & U & T & I & F & U & L \\ -\cdot\cdot & \cdot\cdot- & - & \cdot\cdot & & & \text{(same)} \end{array}$$

This shows how easily Morse can be misread by an inexperienced operator, and it is against mistakes of this kind that the code compilers had to guard in forming their series of words.

It was not until 1903 that code words were allowed only ten characters, and had to be pronounceable to be authorized for transmission at the cost of plain text words.

In 1904 Whitelaw's Telegraph Ciphers appeared with 400 million pronounceable words. It was not a code book at all, but merely a list of artificial pronounceable words that could be used for private codes. These code words were composed of five letters only, for example FORAB, LUFFA, LOZOJ, etc., as are all words used in commercial codes to-day.

Twenty-thousand words of five letters each were given, and since each was pronounceable, and any two of these words could be joined together to form a group chargeable according to telegraph regulations as one word, so 20,000 squared gave the total of potential words as 400 millions.

In 1906 Bentley's code appeared, a compact phrase code based on five-letter groups, applicable to business affairs in general. It had a great success, as the cost of any message, even if encoded verbatim, could be cut down by half.

These artificial five-letter groups, any two of which could form one ten-letter word authorized for telegraph transmission, could be transmitted far more accurately than the old style dictionary word, and these new codes quickly replaced the old ones.

Morse

Let us now consider the man who gave his name to a code which is in use throughout the world to-day. Samuel Finley Breese Morse was born in 1791 in Charlestown, Mass., U.S.A. He was the eldest son of a clergyman, and after taking his degree at Yale University he became an artist. He was always keenly interested in electrical science, then in its infancy. He studied painting in London and Paris and obtained some recognition, receiving a gold medal from the Adelphi Society of Arts in London; but he abandoned painting after he was rejected as one of the artists to be commissioned to paint some pictures for the Capitol in Washington, through a personal misunderstanding with ex-President Adams. Returning to America in 1832, he discussed with a friend he met on board ship the question of transmitting electric current through great lengths of wire, and there and then conceived the idea of electrical telegraphy.

This invention had to undergo many vicissitudes before it arrived at a practical stage. Nobody thought it could be of any financial value, and it was only in 1843 that the United States Congress voted $35,000 for the construction of the first telegraph line between Washington and Baltimore. Morse then applied for a patent in England, which was refused on a very feeble pretext, and at the same time his other European patents were violated. Various lawsuits were started in America which were not finally settled in his favour until 1854. But he eventually achieved universal recognition. Napoleon III started a Gratitude Fund for him to which almost all European countries subscribed, and it reached the total of 400,000 francs. This gift was all the more valuable to him as at that time he was in serious financial difficulties. It was not until he was over sixty that his services were fully recognized.

Our chief interest in Morse lies in 'Morse Code', which he based actually on the frequency of letters, calculated on quantities of type found in a printing office. As it is the frequency tables which are of such an enormous help in deciphering every code, we compare here the original calculation made by Morse with the Normal Frequency and the Telegraph Frequency.

COMMERCIAL CODES

		Actual number of letters found by Morse at his Printers	Order of Normal Frequency
E	1st	12,000	1st
T	2nd	9,000	2nd
A	3rd	8,000	4th
I	3rd	8,000	6th
N	3rd	8,000	5th
O	3rd	8,000	3rd
S	3rd	8,000	8th
H	4th	6,400	9th
R	5th	6,200	7th
D	6th	4,400	10th
L	7th	4,000	11th
U	8th	3,400	12th
C	9th	3,000	13th
M	9th	3,000	14th
F	10th	2,500	16th
W	11th	2,000	18th
Y	11th	2,000	17th
G	12th	1,700	19th
P	12th	1,700	15th
B	13th	1,600	20th
V	14th	1,200	21st
K	15th	800	22nd
Q	16th	500	26th
J	17th	400	23rd
X	17th	400	24th
Z	18th	200	25th

Comparative Table of Order of Morse's Count with Telegraph Frequencies

       1st 2nd   3rd   4th 5th 6th 7th 8th   9th

Morse : E, T, A, I, N, O, S, H, R, D, L, U, C͡, M,
Telegraph : E, O, A, N, I, R, S, T, D, H, L, U,

       10th   11th   12th 13th 14th 15th 16th 17th 18th

Morse : F, W͡, Y͡, G͡, P, B, V, K, Q͡, J, X, Z.
Telegraph : C, M, P, Y, F, G, W, B, V, K, X, J, Q, Z,

For the letters which were most frequent he used the simplest combination of dots and dashes, which an automatic contrivance of the electric current alternately transmitted and suspended during longer or shorter intervals and reproduced at the other end of the wire on strips of paper. An experienced operator does not need to read the strips, but can read the message by ear, the variations in the clicking of the magnet being sufficient for his trained ear to differentiate between the dots and the dashes.

The Morse code is used not only in telegraphy but also in signalling by flags, by flashes of light, and by long and short blasts from a whistle.

Our army regulations allow ten days to the recruit signallers to learn the Morse code, but here is a method which, it is claimed, enables any one to learn it in an hour. It is simply a list of words, one for each letter of the alphabet, the long and short syllables indicating dashes and dots. This method was invented by Morse himself for use in the U.S. Army.

		Morse			Morse
A.	Ag-ainst	. −	N.	Nob-le	− .
B.	Bar-ba-ri-an	− . . .	O.	Off-ens-ive	− − −
C.	Cont-in-ent-al	− . − .	P.	Pho-tog-raph-er	. − − .
D.	Dah-li-a	− . .	Q.	Queen Ka-tha-rine	− − . −
E.	(short)	.	R.	Re-bec-ca	. − .
F.	Fu-ri-ous-ly	. . − .	S.	Se-ver-al	. . .
G.	Gal-lant-ly	− − .	T.	Tea	−
H.	Hu-mi-li-ty	. . . .	U.	Un-i-form	. . −
I.	I-vy	. .	V.	Ve-ry va-ried	. . . −
J.	Ju-ris-dic-tion	. − − −	W.	Wa-ter-loo	. − −
K.	Kan-ga-roo	− . −	X.	Ex-hi-bi-tion	− . . −
L.	Le-gis-la-tor	. − . .	Y.	Youth-ful and fair	− . − −
M.	Moun-tain	− −	Z.	(two long, two short)	− − . .

It will be observed that each of these words contains as many syllables as there are dots and dashes in the corresponding Morse equivalent; but owing to the difficulty of finding suitable words, it was assumed that vowels followed by two or more letters are long and those followed by one letter are short. In the words 'Katharine' and 'offensive', for instance, the final syllable must be considered long.

These words can be learned in a very few minutes and by their means the knowledge of Morse can be carried in one's head; each word contains within itself the essential characteristic of a Morse letter, and suggests by its initial its place in the alphabet. It will be a great help if the following sentences are memorized:

GALLANTLY and FURIOUSLY he fought AGAINST the foe at WATERLOO.

IVY creeping along the ground suggests HUMILITY.

The JURISDICTION of the NOBLE LEGISLATOR was offensive to the BARBARIAN.

A PHOTOGRAPHER saw SEVERAL KANGAROOS on the MOUNTAIN.

Commercial Codes

Generally speaking, commercial codes are used not so much for secrecy as for saving money on long telegrams, an authorized, pronounceable word of the maximum length of ten letters being used to cover several sentences. The words are, of course, entirely fictitious, and in the commercial codes they follow each other in alphabetical order, being made up of five letters each, so that two code words can be sent by telegraph for the price of one word.

Here is an example of ABC Code (English only):

Code No.	Half Code Word	Meaning
00000	ABAAA	'ABC' Code (*see also* sentences under Codes)
00001	ABADE	Please use 'ABC' Code 6th Edition
00002	ABAEF	Please use 'ABC' Code 6th Edition and Code - - - - - (s)
00003	ABAFG	Please use 'ABC' Code 6th Edition and private Code
00004	ABAGH	Using 'ABC' Code 6th Edition
00005	ABAHI	Using 'ABC' Code 6th Edition and Code - - - - - - - -
00006	ABAIJ	Abandon (*see also*: discontinue, forgo, give up)
00007	ABAJK	Abandon altogether
00008	ABAKL	Abandon for the present
00009	ABALM	Abandon or (- - -)
00010	ABAMN	Abandon the action

It is interesting to compare the formation of the five-letter half code words used in the ABC Code with those used by the Marconi, an example of which is given on p. 82.

Other codes constructed on these principles are Bentley's and Webster's. They all allow two words, or even two short sentences sometimes, to be formed into one telegraph word of ten letters.

Not only is a considerable economy achieved by the use of a code, but the ancient philosophers' and cabbalists' dream has at last been realized. There are commercial codes to-day with equivalent translations into every European language, so that English, German, or Italian business men, without knowing each other's languages, can exchange telegrams.

They are very simple to use, and the telegraph companies, instead of prohibiting them, have welcomed and simplified them so as to attract more business. The growth in the use of telegraph and cables for business purposes during the last decade shows how well this policy has paid.

Marconi

Senator Guglielmo Marconi had an Italian father and an Irish-Scots mother. He was born in Bologna, in Italy, in 1874. His father was a well-to-do man of affairs, and in Marconi we have, for once, not only an inventor who devoted the whole of his life to his one idea, the sending and receiving of wireless signals through space, having started investigating this question when still a schoolboy, but also one who did not have to struggle in poverty, who was well connected in society, well educated, and did not meet with any difficulties, apart from those of a technical nature, in launching his invention on the world. He did this before he was twenty-one—that is, as soon as he succeeded in persuading his father, a hard-headed business man, that his invention was a really sound one and had a practical application.

Marconi was the best example of a man with one single idea dominating his whole life. He disliked meeting strangers and detested having to talk for the sake of talking, although he was not naturally shy. As he did not lack money, he was not forced to ingratiate himself with men of substance and power; and perhaps this independence made others desire his company and friendship, and enabled him to command his associates' complete devotion and loyalty throughout their lifetime. He had three or four friends who were devoted to him; they all had the same interests and shared his faith in his own invention before it was recognized by the world.

When he first achieved fame, after the practical tests made by the British G.P.O. in London in 1896, newspapers started to 'front page' him, but he assiduously refused to be lionized, and, to the disappointment of some of his friends, refused the most pressing social invitations.

He had great difficulties with the German government, which shamelessly copied his early patents, so that for a long time German ships were not allowed to communicate with Marconi-equipped ships. But it was with a telegraph company that he had most trouble. They held an exclusive charter for telegraphic communication with Newfoundland, and when Marconi put up a station of his own there and experimented with his wireless signals, they threatened him with a lawsuit. So he packed up his apparatus and returned to Italy, taking good care that the public should know of the incident. And public opinion was very much incensed with the procedure of the company.

Next, at the invitation of the Canadian government, he set up a station in Canada, and was able to experiment there successfully, obtaining for the first time wireless signals across the Atlantic.

Through all these vicissitudes, and in spite of the fact that he lost an eye in a motor accident in 1912, Marconi preserved an almost Chinese composure, and calmly carried on with his tests, showing an uncanny foreknowledge of his ultimate success.

Before his death in 1938 he had received the highest honours from every European state. In his own country he was created a Marquis; but, in spite of wealth and fame, he lived alone with his wife, an Irishwoman, on board his yacht *Elletra*, which he fitted up as a floating laboratory and where he worked on wireless inventions right up to his death.

Marconi Codes

The complete Marconi code consists of four volumes comprising English, Spanish, Japanese, Russian, Italian,

Portuguese, German, and Dutch equivalents. The English text is alphabetical, but every other language has a complete index of all the words. The code is divided into two parts—one containing general phrases and the other a numeral system.

As has been already said, the chief aim of a standard code is to save cost of cable charges and cost of time required to code messages. Upwards of 17,050 combinations can be obtained by the Marconi code. A checking system ensures accuracy.

The code words are composed of five letters each, and each code word corresponds either to a word or a short sentence usual in trade or commerce. Two of such code words are joined together to form a telegraph word of ten letters allowed by the International Telegraph regulations.

Each code word has a two-letter difference from every other code word. This two-letter difference ensures that no two words can have the same four letters in the same position. Such a code word as BOPEZ, for instance, eliminates code words such as COPEZ, DOPEZ, BAPEZ, BEPEZ.

The Numeral System is so arranged that a range of figures in combination with some of the most commonly used qualifying phrases, together with an efficient check, can be transmitted in one complete pronounceable code word of ten letters.

The first syllable in this section always consists of two consonants, thereby distinguishing it from a phrase section in which none of the code words begins with two consonants. As the code words in the numeral system are composed of two letters only, five words or sentences can be included in one telegraph word of ten letters.

F

The arrangement is as follows:

1*st Syllable* provides for a variety of phrases which may be employed in combination with the figures or phrases in the following syllables, described as 'qualifying phrases'; e.g., 'TH' = remit by cable, 'TW' = ship immediately.

2*nd Syllable* provides for an extensive variety of phrases descriptive of the following weights and measures; e.g., 'OM' = pounds, 'WG' = tons.

3*rd Syllable* provides for figures from fractions to 100.

4*th Syllable* provides for more figures to be used in conjunction with the third syllable. If unnecessary a 'blank' must be used here, or short phrase to qualify, such as 'ZA' = per month.

5*th Syllable* provides for a further series of phrases to be used in conjunction with the foregoing; e.g., 'AL' = for immediate shipment. It also supplies a check for the whole coded word.

The first part of the Marconi Code. General phrases, Code words, five letters.

Number	Code Word	English	French	Spanish
00000	ABABA	A or an	un, une	un, uno, una
00001	ABAHB	A1 at Lloyd's	A1 chez Lloyd's	A1 en el registro de Lloyd
00002	ABALC	Abandon(s)	Abandonne(r) (z)	Abandona(r) (u)
00003	ABAND	Abandon all claims	Abandonne toutes réclamations	Abandona todas las reclamaciones
00004	ABAPE	Abandon negotiations	Abandonne les négociations	Abandona las negociaciones
00005	ABARF	Abandon proceedings	Abandonne les démarches	Abandona los procedimientes

etc.

Numeral System. Code word of two letters.
1st Syllable.

Check No. in red	Code Syllable	English	French	Spanish
(0)	BL	Blank or At	Blanc ou À	Blanco o A
(5)	BR	Bid (they)	Ils offrent	ofrecen
(8)	CH	Bid (we)	Nous offrons	ofrecemos
(1)	CL	Bought (we have)	Nous avons acheté	Hemos comprado
(6)	CR	Breadth (or thickness)	Largeur (ou épaisseur) etc.	Anchura (o espesura)

2nd Syllable.

		English	French	Spanish
(5)	AB	Blank	Blanc	Blanco
(6)	AC	Acre(s)	Acre(s)	Acre(s)
(7)	AD	Ampere(s)	Ampère(s)	Amperio(s)
(8)	AF	Anna(s)	Anna(s)	Anna(s)
(9)	AG	Ante Meridian (A.M.)	Matin, avant midi etc.	Antes de mediodía (A.M.)

3rd Syllable.

(5)	AB	Blank	Blanc	Blanco
(6)	AC	0	0	0
(7)	AD	1/16	1/16	1/16
(8)	BI	1	1	1
(7)	BO	1/14	1/14 etc.	1/14

4th Syllable.

(9)	YA	000	000	000
(0)	YB	100	100	100
(1)	YC	200	200	200
(1)	YM	per annum	par an	por año
(2)	YN	per centimetre	par centimètre etc.	por centimetro

5th Syllable. Control of check.

	0	1	2	3	4	5	6	7	8	9
Blank	..	..	AR	EN	BU	HI	JA	NA	OY	TO	VA	YG
About	..	..	AC	EP	BY	HO	JE	NE	OZ	TU	VE	YH
Average	..	..	AD	ER	CA	HU	JI	NI	PA	TY	VI	YI
C.I.F. (Cost Insurance Freight)	..	..	AF	ES	CE	HY	JO	NO	PE	WB	VO	YJ
each	..	..	AG	ET	CI	IB	JU	NU	PI	UC	VU	YK

etc.

84   CODES AND CIPHERS

The checking system is very simple. The check numbers given in brackets on each code syllable are added together for the four syllables used; tens are disregarded, and for the fifth syllable the letters are chosen from the column bearing the same number as the total arrived at from the addition of the first four syllables.

The other codes chiefly used in commerce are Bentley's and Webster's.

Shorthand

In the study of secret language used in trade and commerce we have to consider shorthand, which plays such a great part in business to-day.

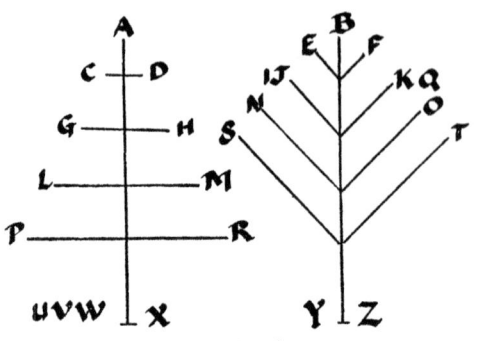

Tree Alphabet

Stenography or Tachygraphy (Gk. *takhus+graphein*) was first used in A.D. 195 in a letter by Flavius Philostratus; all the earlier instances are controversial. The origin of Greek tachygraphy probably grew out of a system of secret writing developed from forms of abbreviations used by the early Christians.

Tyronian 'notae', of which mention was made in the first chapter, must of course be considered as a form of shorthand, however clumsy and complicated it was. Nevertheless, it

COMMERCIAL CODES 85

was used by the church right up to the eleventh century, as well as by advocates and jurists. Hence the name 'notaries'. In England we find the first mention of Tyronian 'notae' in 1180, when a certain John Tilbury wrote an *Epistle on Notarial Art*, in which he also mentions the 'tree' alphabet of Dioscorides which was apparently used by the Phoenicians. It is based on designs which resemble trees.

As far as we know, until the sixteenth century the art of shorthand was in abeyance, and it was only when Timothy Bright, 'Doctor of Phisike', published his book called *The Arte of Shorte, Swifte and Secrete Writing* in 1588 that shorthand as we understand the term had its beginning. It is curious to note the extent to which all modern systems of shorthand have copied the 'Doctor of Phisike's' characters.

Bright's Characters

But although Bright invented the alphabet, his system was not an alphabetical one—it was really a kind of hieroglyphic method. 'Labour', for instance, was the same as L with an added tail, whilst two dots on the other side made it into 'labourer'.

Altogether the student had to learn some six hundred different characters, which had no relation to the alphabet, and certain words were expressed only by their two initial letters; e.g., 'shackles', 'shade', 'shadow', 'shake', etc., were all written as SH.

Nevertheless, it was less complicated than Tyronian 'notae', and marked a definite advance in the art of stenography, which began to improve steadily from that time.

In 1602 John Willis published the first alphabetical system. Although it was not actually published until the seventeenth century it was in constant use before that, as the author states himself. From that time onwards we can distinguish three different kinds of shorthand:

1. Alphabetical or the ABC method, invented by Taylor and published in 1786.
2. Phonetic method, of which various systems were published from 1750 (Tiffin) to 1819 (De Stains).
3. The Phonographic method, of which the chief exponent if not the actual inventor was Isaac Pitman, who first published his system in 1837.

ABC systems. Each letter is designed by a straight line or curve (vertical, horizontal, or sloping); 'k' is substituted both for hard 'c' and 'g', and 's' for soft 'c', and special signs are provided for 'ch', 'sh', 'th'; while 'g' and 'j', 'f' and 'v', 's' and 'z' have one sign for each pair.

It is of interest to note that Samuel Pepys used the Shelton system in his Diary (1620), and that the advertisement of that system in the *Political Mercury Journal* of October, 1650, is probably the first commercial advertisement to have appeared in England.

Another curious incident is that in 1740 Thomas Gurney published the Mason system of shorthand. Shortly afterwards Gurney brought out a new edition, which was a great improvement on the original system. In 1757 his son, B. Gurney, was appointed shorthand writer to the Old Bailey, and another descendant, W. Gurney, was appointed in 1802 to a similar post in the House of Commons. Messrs. Gurney are still the official shorthand writers to the Houses of Parliament, the hereditary tenure of the office remaining unbroken for nearly 150 years.

John Byrom published, in 1767, a very good method of shorthand, and until Isaac Pitman published his 'phonographic' method, it was generally accepted as the best.

We give a description of Pitman's system as being representative of its kind, and one that is widely used.

Pitman's System. Sounds 'p', 't', 'ch', and 'k' are expressed by \ | / __ respectively, and the corresponding 'b', 'd', 'j', 'g' the same but heavily written, thus \ | / __. 'F', 'th' (as in 'thing'), 's', and 'sh' are indicated by ⌒ ( ) ⌡. The same signs written heavily and tapering are used for 'v', 'th' (as in 'thou'), 'z', and 'zh'. 'M', 'n', 'l', 'r' are denoted by ⌒⌣⌒⌐. 'R' is also represented by ╱ written upwards and more slanting than 'ch'. 'W', 'y', 'h' are ╱ ╱ ╱ all upwards, but 'h' is also written down ⟩. Simple 's' is generally written ○.

Long vowels of 'a' (as in 'father'), 'a' (as in 'day'), and 'ee' are marked by a heavy dot placed respectively at the beginning, middle, and end of a consonant sign. 'Aw, oh, oo' by a heavy dash in the same three positions and at right angles to the consonant sign.

Short vowels of 'a' (as in pat), 'e' (as in pet), 'i' (as in pit), 'o' (as in pot), 'u' (as in but) and 'oo' (as in put) are the same as the corresponding long vowels but are written lightly. The signs for 'ei' (as in bite) or 'ow' (as in cow) are $\vee$ and $\wedge$ and may be placed in any position with regard to the consonant.

Pitman's shorthand must be written on lined paper while some of the others need not be. Although Everett's system published in 1877 has been generally accepted as the best and broadly speaking is more of a phonetic system than Pitman's the latter is still in general use. The Sloan-Duployan (1882) system is a little more complicated, but it must be mentioned as in America almost all the systems employed are phonetical. They are best suited for verbatim reporting, but to be legible must be written with care. The usual speed of writing is about 120 words a minute, but some people have been known to speak as rapidly as 180 and even 200 words per minute.

CHAPTER V
MILITARY CODES AND CIPHERS

CRYPTOGRAPHY is used to a large extent by the army, which not only provides some training for cipher officers but has evolved certain methods suitable for military purposes.

Under modern conditions every large army unit has cipher officers on the staff, whose sole duty it is to encode or decode telegrams or other messages. But within the military organization of any European country to-day the place where cryptography flourishes is the Intelligence Department.

In the Intelligence Department of any army, information about the enemy is received, collated, and passed on to the executives—generals, commanding officers, and operations staff. Part of the Intelligence Department actually deals with the Secret Service, about which so many romantic stories have been written.

This is an organization dealing with spies in the enemy countries, who in peace-time obtain secret information about troops, details of equipment, new weapons, changes in the military organization, and so on, while in war-time the spy tries to get hold of plans of operations, position, number and movements of enemy troops.

Another part of the Secret Service is counter-espionage, which deals with the discovery and suppression of enemy spies in one's own country. In most European armies this department has a sub-branch which is solely engaged in breaking the coded or ciphered messages found on enemy spies, or caught in transmission.

I heard once of an ingenious code used during the war of 1914-18 by a 'transmitter' spy, that is, a person whose only duty is to pass on the information to others. He was suspected, and watch was kept on a newspaper kiosk he owned. But for a long time it could not be discovered who collected the information, or how it was handed on. One day it was observed that during the course of the morning he changed the order of the newspapers which were stuck in a rack outside his shop. He had a whole row of different newspapers and magazines on a grille outside the door, and it was the order in which these papers were displayed that constituted the code he used to transmit the secret messages to his confederate, who did not have to go inside the shop, which might have led to suspicion, but just noted from outside the order of the displayed newspapers, and went on his way without any one being the wiser.

Leakage of important military information may be occasioned in several ways. Informers may sell it to enemy spies; it may be unintentionally revealed in gossip, or indiscreet conversations on field telephones; soldiers may give away secrets in their letters from the front; and troops may be identified by their badges.

German Army Ciphers

The Germans are reputed to pay far more attention to ciphers than any other country. They were the first to give a special course in cryptography to young subalterns, and practically every German officer is fully conversant with the theory and current practice of ciphers.

The majority of books on this subject have been written by Germans, who have invented many adaptations of old ciphers.

For communications between divisional staffs and higher command the Germans had a cipher table based on the same principle as on p. 91, but more complicated and using letters instead of figures.

MILITARY CODES AND CIPHERS

GERMAN ARMY CIPHER

	2nd figure	3	6	0	7	4	8	1	9	5	2
1st figure	2	a	ä	ai	au	aü	b	c	ch	ck	d
	6	e	ei	eu	f	ff	g	h	i	ie	j
	3	k	l	ll	m, mm	n, nn	o	ö	p	pp	r
	7	s	sch	sp	spr	ss	st	str	t	tt	u
	4	ü	v	w	x	y	z	o	1	2	3
	0	4	5	6	7	8	9	.	,	;	?
	8	section	army	artillery	Battalion	Battery	Brigade	bridge	Division	railway	squadron
	1	field	flight	flying corps	engineers	rifles	trench mortars	group	infantry	scouts	guns
	9	cavalry	company	command	corps	men	morse	munitions	officer	horse	pioneer
	5	regiment	Red Cross	snipers	sappers	staff	tanks	train	troop	watch	balloons

Example:

Message: Three Companies to attack bridge-head at once.
Plain text: 3 Companies t o a t t a ck bridge h e a d a t o n c e .
Cipher: 42   96,   79, 38, 23, 75, 23, 25,   81,   61, 63, 23, 22, 22,   23, 79, 38, 34,   21, 63, 01.
Cryptogram: 42967 93823 75232 58161 63232 22379 38342 16301

91

Major Schneickerts, who was in charge of the German spies in Russia before the war of 1914-18, used a very simple numerical cipher, which changed every day of the year. The following message was intercepted from one of his agents:

Mr. Herz offers from Ladoga the following timber :
Pine wood timbers .. 143 wagons at 5 roubles 31 copecks p.w.
Walnut battens .. 251 ,, ,, 11 ,, 8 ,, ,,
Pine wood planks .. 111 ,, ,, 4 ,, 21 ,, ,,
White wood poles .. 242 ,, ,, 2 ,, 14 ,, ,,
Walnut planks .. 242 ,, ,, 11 ,, 13 ,, ,,
White wood laths .. 132 ,, ,, 3 ,, 82 ,, ,,
Odd white wood
 timber .. .. 132 ,, ,, 3 ,, 22-91 ,, ,,

Freight 43 copecks ton/klm. or 62 cop. delivered, loading 41 cop. per ton, delivery 32 roubles per wagon 3 weeks to 2 months from order. Stilman has bought:

White wood .. .. 63 wagons at 6 roubles 36 copecks
White wood posts.. .. 352 ,, ,, 4 ,, 35 ,,

The figures in that message constitute the cipher, and it was quite easy to find the key which was as follows:

	A	B	C	D	E	F	G	H	I	J	K	L	M
Cipher :	21	27	12	29	35	19	26	36	11	28	37	18	25
	N	O	P	Q	R	S	T	U	V	W	X	Y	Z
Cipher :	31	13	38	17	24	32	14	23	33	16	34	22	15

I will leave the interested reader to work out the message for himself.

The German Spy Müller

The late Sir Basil Thomson had a very interesting story to tell about the capture of Müller, who was shot in the Tower of London. He came to England pretending to be a refugee from Russia, and sent valuable information to Germany in letters written in secret inks. These the police were lucky enough to intercept. One day a letter was collected bearing a Deptford postmark, saying that 'C' had gone to Newcastle and that the writer would receive information at 201.

Sir Basil found on investigating that there was only one street in Deptford in which the houses were numbered to 201. That house was a bakery, kept by a man of German extraction. When it was searched, similar paper and secret inks were found in the shop, and 'C' was identified as Müller. He was arrested in Newcastle, tried, and sentenced to death.

The Secret Service used all this to their advantage. They copied Müller's handwriting and methods and 'fed' false information to the Germans for over three months before it was discovered by their spies that Müller was dead.

During the years previous to the war of 1914-18, when every secret service in the world was occupied in trying to discover the strength and weakness of the others, a number

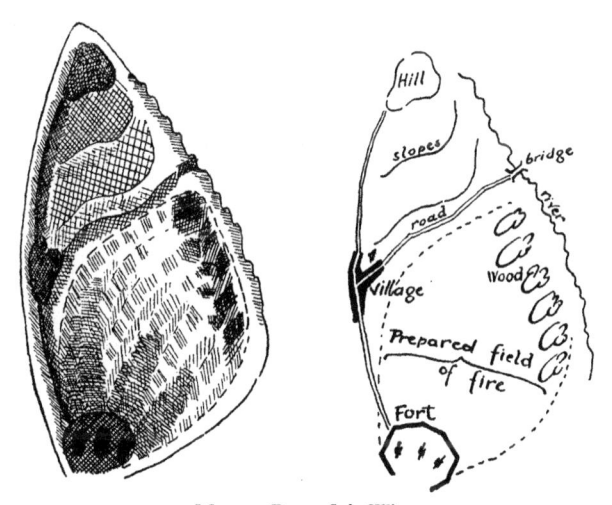

Map on Butterfly's Wing

of German naturalists appeared on the French frontier, examining the plant and animal life of the district and collecting specimens. Some of these young men were active with butterfly nets, and all of them were adept at making beautiful drawings of leaves and butterflies' wings. But the French were quick to observe peculiar markings on some of the butterfly wings, and the young scientists were quickly suppressed.

One of the drawings and its interpretation from the military point of view is reproduced.

The three guns in the fort give the strength of the artillery. The scale denotes limits to the field of fire, the distance from a hill, and the position of a bridge over a river. You can see yourself how drawings of leaves and flowers could be made to convey similar details.

French Army

Apart from the various books on cryptography, and very clever scientific methods evolved by Vesin de Romanini,

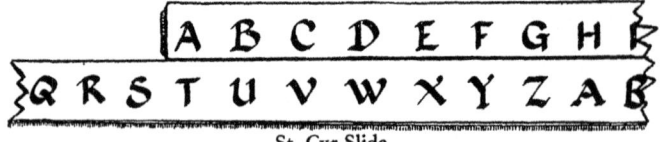

```
| A B C D E F G H |
| Q R S T U V W X Y Z A |
```
St. Cyr Slide

Bazeries, Kerckhoff, Josse, and others for the deciphering of codes without a key, the official cryptographic methods in France until recent times were not as thorough or as efficient as those of the Germans.

Their military ciphers were based on either St. Cyr slides, an adaptation of the Vigénère cipher (see Chapter II); or on a system adopted by the French Admiralty in 1870 and in its turn based on an invention of M. Auvray, which has since

MILITARY CODES AND CIPHERS 95

been used by many other nations for their diplomatic correspondence. It uses the following principles:

1st Alphabet

Plain text :	A	B	C	D	E	F	G	H	I	J	K	L	M
Cipher :	1	2	3	4	5	6	7	8	9	10	11	12	13
Plain text :	N	O	P	Q	R	S	T	U	V	W	X	Y	Z
Cipher :	14	15	16	17	18	19	20	21	22	23	24	25	26

2nd Alphabet

(Same as the preceding but starting with 101, 102, 103, and so on.)
Example : *Key* : Honour in 2nd Alphabet = 108, 115, 114, 115, 121, 118.

Message : Enemy moves east.

Keyword :	H	O	N	O	U	R	H	O	N	O
2nd Alphabet :	108	115	114	115	121	118	108	115	114	115
Plain text :	E	n	e	m	y	m	o	v	e	s
1st Alphabet :	5	14	5	13	25	13	15	22	5	19
Cryptogram :	103	101	109	102	96	105	93	93	109	96
Keyword :	U	R	H	O						
2nd Alphabet :	121	118	108	115						
Plain text :	e	a	s	t						
1st Alphabet :	5	1	19	20						
Cryptogram :	116	117	89	95						

(The numbers in the crypt are arrived at by subtraction of the 1st alphabet from the 2nd.)

Another system used in France at one time was based on the so-called Cronfeld method. It consists of irregular substitution.

Reference Alphabet : A, b, c, d, e, f, g, h, i, j, k, l, m, n, o, p, q, r, s, t, u, etc.

Key : ..	3 5 1 3 2	3 5 1 3 2	3 5 1 3 2 3	Message :
Plain text :	B R I G A	D E M O V	E S A W A Y	Brigade
Cryptogram :	e w j j c	g j n r x	h x b z c b	moves away.

The cryptogram is enciphered by first of all writing the figures of the agreed key over the letters of the plain text. Then, using the reference alphabet, one counts from the letter B of the plain text three letters to the right, which gives E. The figure 3 is of course given by the key which is written above the plain text. In the same manner, counting five letters from R in the plain text we get W, and the first letter from 'I' in the plain text is J, etc.

This cipher has one disadvantage, however—it is very easy to make a mistake in counting the letters, and this alone might upset the whole meaning of the message. As it is, messages very often get mutilated in transmission. The ideal cipher is one that is simple for those who use it and difficult for anybody else.

A very good example of mutilation is that with which young subalterns probably still amuse each other in the mess. A battalion was being trained in the oral transmission of a message along the line from one man to another. The original message was: 'Enemy concentrating, send reinforcements.' After some six hundred men had had their say about it, it arrived as: '' 'Enery constipated, send three and fourpence.'

British Army Ciphers

At the Battle of Waterloo, it will be remembered, the British infantry was drawn up in hollow square formation, and the victory of our army on that occasion was due to the fact that the squares were able to withstand the violent shocks of the French charges throughout the day. Though battered, the squares remained unbroken. Many other British victories have been achieved in the same way, and in fact the hollow square may be regarded as a peculiarly British contribution to military tactics. It is interesting, therefore, to discover that

MILITARY CODES AND CIPHERS 97

the majority of British military ciphers were also based on the square, of which Lord Wolseley's is a very good example.

In the *Soldier's Pocket Book* he has given us a very simple square cipher for use under active service conditions. It has been used with modifications since the beginning of this century. Here it is:

1. Divide a square into 25 spaces and number them. The method of numbering them and the keyword are all that one has to remember, so that when a message in cipher is received, one has only to draw a square as below, and number the divisions in the same way. The keyword can be changed daily or whenever necessary. The only rule about the keyword is that it should be a word of at least six or seven letters, and must not have any letter repeated in it.

1 M	2 A	3 J(I)	4 E	5 S
8 T	9 Y	10 B	11 C	6 D
7 F	12 G	H	12 K	7 L
6 N	11 O	10 P	9 Q	8 R
5 U	4 V	3 W	2 X	1 Z

In the diagram the word 'Majesty' is the key; the letters composing it are accordingly spelled along the spaces from left to right, beginning at the left-hand top corner. The succeeding spaces are filled with the remaining letters of the alphabet in their proper sequence. For instance, in the above example, after the 'Y' of 'majesty' the next letter is 'B', because 'A' is in the key word and 'B' is not; then 'C', 'D' and 'F' ('E' being in the keyword) and so on to 'Z'.

In this and all other ciphers, whether letters or figures be used, they should be written in groups of four or five, so that, while giving no clue to the length of the words used, the accidental omission of letters or figures may be more easily detected. This is especially necessary when the messages are transmitted by signals or electric telegraph.

Messages are written in this cipher as follows: take the first letter of the message, note the number of the square containing that letter, and substitute the letter in the other square with the same number; and so on for each letter.

Thus, if I want to send the following message, 'We attack at noon', it would run thus in the cipher:

JVXR RXOG XRDC CDDD

It may be seen that there are two more letters in the cipher message than in the actual words of the message; these two letters are to bring the last group up to four, which would otherwise have only two letters in it. In adding letters for this purpose, care must be taken to select those that are least liable to lead to misinterpretation. One letter will always be in the unnumbered square, and when it occurs in a message the true letter must be used. With 'majesty' for a keyword, that letter is 'H'. To decipher a message the process is merely the reverse of that described above.

This cipher is of course easily made out, but if every third, fourth, or fifth letter, as may be previously arranged, is a dummy inserted after a message has been put into cipher, it is then extremely difficult to decipher unless you are in the secret.

MILITARY CODES AND CIPHERS 99

General Army Rules for Cipher Messages

We give these rules here as they will facilitate the handling of ciphers generally and give an indication of the usual military procedure with ciphers.

In case of an alphabetical or figure cipher being handed in for transmission, the signaller will at once split up that portion of the message which is in cipher into groups of five letters or numerals as the case may be, the odd letters or numerals forming a group by themselves.

A cipher sign such as CC preceding and following the cipher group shows that a letter cipher has been used; the letters CCFI stand for a figure cipher. Should a group be incorrectly repeated, the sending station will immediately signal the 'erase', which will be answered by the 'erase', and it will then repeat the group.

Example 1. Letter cipher : 'I will arrange for (CC) XYKCD MQRAD GVK (CC) and after that (CC) XZALG MSAQW QAL (CC) Instructions requested.'

Example 2. Figure cipher : 'I will arrange for (CCFI) 23301 89972 41 (CC) and after that (CCFI) 29330 61100 465 (CC) Instructions requested.'

According to the *Book on Army Signals in the Field*, it seldom happens that a message is composed entirely of cipher. More frequently the latter occurs at intervals, and in such cases only those portions of the message actually in cipher must be arranged in groups of five letters or figures. The sets of five should be marked off by short vertical lines so as to simplify the sending and counting of each group.

We give below an example from the Army Signal Book, which best explains the methods used.

To : G.O.C. Cav. Bde., Alton

Day of month	Senders No.	In reply to No.		
20th	14	32	Be	prepared
to	(CC)QNS	BL/KV	QSA/H	QNVX/
RGBF	L/KVX	PZ/TN	(CC) and	report
where	(CC)FKN	XQ/AC	DFK/S	SMON/M
ONSJ/Q	ZB(CC)	detachment	must	retire
on	(CC)VC	ZLN/G	AAA	

From : GSO Aldershot

(Cav. Bde. abbreviation used for Cavalry Brigade.)

The total number of words in the above message is 29, and the cipher groups to be sent are :

QNSBL | KVQSA | HQNVX | RGBFL | KVXPZ | TNFKN
XQACD | FKSS | M/ONM | ON/SJQ | ZB/VCZ | LN/G

One should note that AAA signifies the end of the message.

Very little can be said about the modern army ciphers, for obvious reasons. Neither the War Office nor the Foreign Office will let anybody know anything of their ciphers; even the older ones are kept secret because they are occasionally brought into use.

An Episode of the War of 1914-18

After the war of 1914-18 I was told of a curious coincidence which led to a very important discovery. You may

MILITARY CODES AND CIPHERS

remember the 'grille' cipher, the invention of Jerome Cardan, who lived in Italy in the sixteenth century. This consists of an innocent-looking message which has certain words placed at irregular intervals conveying the hidden meaning. To read it, a piece of cardboard with holes cut in it to correspond to the position of the hidden words is placed over the innocent message, and the true meaning appears at a glance.

An improvement on this method is to hide only letters or syllables instead of words. It should be noted that when important communications are sent even in cipher they are usually sent in triplicate or quadruplicate so as to ensure at least one arriving at its destination.

In the Baltic States, immediately after the war, a good deal of various political and military activity took place. These small states were created as buffers isolating Soviet Russia, and, in consequence, people outside Russia had to communicate with those inside through the territory of these Baltic States.

Obviously these new governments were very suspicious of Russia, and they instituted a very strict censorship of practically all written matter; letters, newspapers, and even books had to undergo an examination by appointed officials. It so happened that one censor noticed that he had read two identical letters written seemingly by two different persons and addressed to two different people in Russia. Very naturally his suspicions were aroused. Why should two different people write exactly identical letters to two different addresses? Note was taken of the addresses, and the letters were photographed. A very much stricter watch than usual was kept. Once again identical letters in the same circumstances turned up, and continued to do so at regular intervals. Note was again taken of them, and then they were sent on to their destination, so as not to arouse the suspicions of the writers. Meanwhile, all the brains of the little state were called in to help to decipher these letters, which had nothing suspicious about them except their complete similarity, even down to the punctuation.

The officials of the new state, being quite inexperienced, were completely baffled, and eventually they called in an old Russian professor, a refugee from the Soviets, to help them. He was said to have been connected at one time with the old Russian Cipher Bureau. He at once decided that a 'grille' had been used, and after many trials, finally deciphered the message. It related to a very active Communist organization supported by the Third International in Moscow. Both the ciphered letters were identical because of the 'grille' employed to hide the secret message, and if it had not been for the coincidence that they had both found their way into the hands of the same censor, probably the fate of that little Baltic State would have been quite different.

CHAPTER VI

TYPES OF CODES AND CIPHERS

IN order to become efficient in the knowledge of codes and ciphers some system of classification must be adopted. As we have already seen, many methods have been employed at different times to preserve secrets from inquiring eyes, and cryptographers throughout the ages have displayed remarkable ingenuity; nevertheless, we can make a few general divisions of ciphers.

1. *Invented Alphabets*, made of arbitrary marks for letters.

The 'Zodiac' alphabet is one of the many types used by the medieval and even earlier cryptographers who wished to hide from the uninitiated their secrets in alchemy, astrology, and philosophy:

A = ☉ = Sun	N = ♌ = Lion
B = ♃ = Jupiter	O = ♍ = Virgo
C = ♄ = Saturn	P = ♎ = Balance (Libra)
D = ♆ = Neptune	Q = ♏ = Scorpion
E = ♅ = Uranus	R = ♐ = Sagittarius
F = ⊕ = Earth	S = ♑ = Capricorn
G = ♀ = Venus	T = ♓ = Fishes
H = ♂ = Mars	U = ♈ = Ram
I = ☿ = Mercury	V = ♒ = Aquarius
J = ☽ = Moon	W = >
K = ♉ = Taurus	X = ≫
L = ♊ = Twins	Y = ⊥
M = ♋ = Cancer	Z = <

103

2. Transposition Ciphers

For instance, the keyword being 'MANCHESTER' (repeated letters must be omitted), the following would be the cipher square:

MANCHESTR
5 1 6 2 4 3 8 9 7

Remaining letters—not in the keyword—are written in the square.

Cipher Square

Letter order :	5	1	6	2	4	3	8	9	7
Keyword :	M	A	N	C	H	E	S	T	R
Remaining alphabet :	B	D	F	G	I	J	K	L	O
	P	Q	U	V	W	X	Y	Z	

The transposed alphabet runs down the columns in the order of numbering—1, 2, 3, and so on. Thus we get:

Plain text :   A B C D E F G H I J K L M N O
Cipher-equivalent :   A D Q C G V E J X H I W M B P
Plain Text :   P Q R S T U V W X Y Z
Cipher-equivalent :   N F U R O S K Y T L Z

Example of enciphering :
     Plain text : ENEMY   ATTACKS   AT   DAWN
     Cipher :   GBGML   AOOAQIR   AO   CAYB

For transmission, the cipher is sent in groups of five letters so that the cryptogram will be:

     GBGML   AOOAQ   IRAOC   AYBZZ ('z' here is a 'null' to complete the five letters).

TYPES OF CODES AND CIPHERS

Ordinary Columnar Transposition of the same kind. The message would be as follows:

    Keyword :   MANCHESTR
    Order of letters :   5 1 6 2 4 3 8 9 7
    Message written thus : ENEMYAT T A
                             CKS ATDAWN
        No. 1 column gives NK
        No. 2 column gives MA
        No. 3 column gives AD, etc.

Enciphered message will be:
        NKMAADYTECESANTATW

Substitution Ciphers

Of these there are an enormous variety, beginning with Biblical ones—writing 'x' instead of 'a', the end letter instead of the first and so on—which are called to-day, when used with a keyword, *'mono-alphabetic substitution'*.

Polyalphabetic systems have a double key.

              2nd letter

	A	B	C	D	E
A	M	A	N	C	H
B	E	S	T	R	B
C	D	F	G	I	K
D	L	O	P	Q	U
E	V	W	X	Y	Z

(1st letter)

Keyword written first. Remaining alphabet follows, J omitted so as to get correct square.
Plain text : ENEMY ATTACKS.
Cipher : BA AC BA AA ED AB BC BC AB AD CE BB.
Cryptogram : BAACB AAAED ABBCB CABAD CEBBE EEEEE
(EE = Z = nulls to finish).

The Vigénère table (given on pp. 136-7) has been modified to give the St. Cyr Slide, (see also p. 94) which resembles a slide-rule but with alphabets instead of numbers:

one alphabet

A	B	C	D	E	F	G	H	etc.
Etc.	U	V	W	X	Y	Z	A	B	C	etc.

two alphabets

The St. Cyr Slides are largely used in France, but in England, at least until very recently, the cipher wheel was used for the purpose of field ciphers in the army (Signalling Instructions, 1896).

Cipher Wheel. The cipher wheel consists of an inner circle round which the letters of the alphabet are placed in the usual order; and an outer circle having the letters of the alphabet in *reversed* order. The disk upon which the former are inscribed is pivoted at its centre; the arm (a) is fixed to the disk at any required letter, say 'A'. The disk is turned round by working the mill head.

In transmitting cipher messages it is necessary that the sender and receiver should work with instruments of identical construction. In the cipher wheel the letters of the *keyword* and those of the *true message* are taken from the *outer ring*; the letters of the *cipher message* being read on the *inner ring*.

Whatever the description of cryptograph used, a keyword (or words), which should consist of at least five or six different letters, is required, and this word must be communicated to those who are likely to wish to use the cipher. To convert a message into cipher:

First, write down the words of the plain text, leaving a small space below each letter.

Cipher Wheel

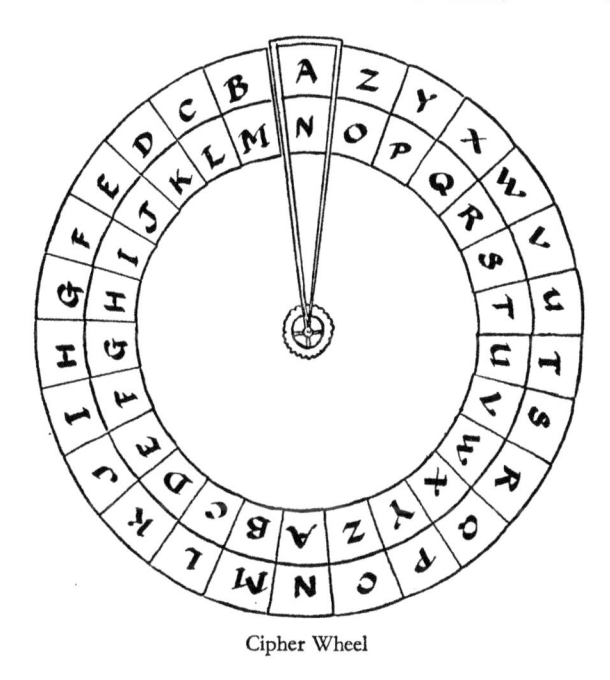

Second, write below the plain text the keyword as often as required.

Third, set the arm of the cipher wheel at the first letter of the keyword (on the outer ring) and take out for the whole message the cipher letters on *the inner ring* corresponding to the plain text on *the outer ring*. Write these down in their places; then move the arm of the cipher wheel to the next letter of the keyword, and proceed as before.

The whole message will be complete as soon as the keyword has been passed once through the arm of the cipher wheel. For example, suppose the true message to be: 'Hold your brigade in readiness to move' and the pre-arranged keyword is 'month'. Write the message with the keyword under it as directed:

```
H o l d y o u r b r i g a d e i n
M O N T H M O N T H M O N T H M O
F A C Q J Y U W S Q E I N Q B E B

r e a d i n e s s t o m o v e
N T H M O N T H M O N T H M O
W P H J G A P P U V Z H T R K
```

(The first line = the text; the second = keyword; the third = cryptogram.)

Turn the arm of the cipher wheel to the letter M, and under the letters HOIID, etc., will be found the letters FYEEJ, etc.; write these down in order, under each of the M's in the key letters. Then turn the arm to the letter O, and under the true letters OUGNI, etc., will be found the cipher letters AUIBG, etc.; write these also in order, under the O's in the key letters, continuing the process till all the letters of the word 'month' are exhausted.

To decipher a message, the reverse of the preceding operation is gone through. Write down the cipher letters with the keyword underneath them, repeated as often as necessary; then turning the arm to the first letter of the keyword *on the outer ring*, read off all the cipher letters *on the inner ring* consecutively, underneath the first key letter. Proceed in the same manner until the whole of the letters of the keyword are finished, when the message, if correctly received, should be completed.

The system of ciphers using a repetition of the keyword is called a 'periodic' system, and such systems may be further classified into progressive alphabet and multiple alphabet systems. In the latter type only a limited number and specific members of the complete set of alphabets contained in the system are used in a single message (see the last example), while in the progressive system all the cipher alphabets pertaining to the system are employed in succession in a single definite sequence, which may be repeated. Such periodicity can be entirely suppressed by introduction of variable elements or interruptions, and each cipher letter may become the key letter for the encipherment of the next plain text letter.

Each letter of the key may be used to encipher a complete word of the plain text and, as the words are irregular in length, periodicity such as that exhibited on the last page is suppressed; or the key may be interrupted; for instance—MONTH/MON/MO/MONT/MONTH; –5–3–2–4–5, etc.

The substitutions given in the first two ciphers are monographic (single letters), but substitution in pairs (digraphic) may be used, such as 'Playfairs', which was once in general use in the field by the army. A *keyword* is required *in which no letter is repeated*, and all the letters of the alphabet which do not occur in the keyword are entered in the spaces of a square with twenty-five subdivisions, I and J being treated as one letter.

With the keyword CLIQUE, the letters would be arranged as follows:

C	L	I(J)	Q	U
E	A	B	D	F
G	H	K	M	N
O	P	R	S	T
V	W	X	Y	Z

The letters of the text are divided up into *pairs*, and equivalents are found for each pair instead of for each letter.

Every pair of letters in the square must be:

(1) *In the same vertical line.* Thus in the example each letter is represented in cipher by that which stands next below it, and the bottom letter by the top one of the same column. For example: DY is represented by MQ.

Or (2) *In the same horizontal line.* Each letter in this case is represented by that which stands next on its right, and the letter on the extreme right by that on the extreme left of the same horizontal line. For example: EF is represented by AE.

Or (3) *At opposite angles of some rectangle.* Here the two letters are represented by the two which stand at the two remaining angles of the rectangle, each by that which is in the same horizontal line with it. For example: CM is represented by QG.

If on dividing the letters of the text into pairs, a pair is found to be composed of the same letter repeated, a dummy letter such as X or Z should be introduced.

If the message to be sent was: 'Expect messenger tomorrow'; when divided into pairs it would be:

ex pe ct me sẋ se ng er to mo rx ro wx
BV OA UO GD RY OD GH BO OP GS XI SP XY

(letters with dots over them are dummies used to divide the pairs); or if written in groups for transmission by signal:

BVOAU OGDRY ODGHB OOPGS XISPX Y

To decipher such a cryptogram the receiver divides it into pairs and from his table finds the equivalent for these pairs, taking the letters immediately above each when they are in the same vertical line; those immediately on the left when on the same horizontal line; and those at opposite angles of the rectangle, when this can be formed.

Combined Substitution-Transposition Cipher

1st Operation–Substitution.
Plain text: Advance brigade to-morrow.
Keyword: MANCHEST(E)R.
Construct square using five letters for double cipher.

2nd letter

	A	B	C	D	E
A	M	A	N	C	H
B	E	S	T	R	B
C	D	F	G	I,J	K
D	L	O	P	Q	U
E	V	W	X	Y	Z

1st letter

Plain text :	A	D	V	A	N	C	E
Cipher :	AB	CA	EA	AB	AC	AD	BA
Plain text :	B	R	I	G	A	D	E
Cipher :	BE	BD	CD	CC	AB	CA	BA
Plain text :	T	O	M	O	R	R	O	W
Cipher :	BC	DB	AA	DB	BD	BD	DB	EB

2nd Operation—Transposition
Transposed cryptogram will be (from 1st column downwards, etc.) :

Key word :	M	A	N	C	H	E	S	T	R
Letter order :	5	1	6	2	4	3	8	9	7
Cipher written across :	A	B	C	A	E	A	A	B	A
	C	A	D	B	A	B	E	B	D
	C	D	C	C	A	B	C	A	B
	A	B	C	D	B	A	A	D	B
	B	D	B	D	D	B	E	B	D*

* 'D' is a 'null' to complete the square

BADBD	ABCDD	ABBAB
EAABD	ACCAB	CDCCB
ADBBD	AECAE	BBADE

If need be this can be again brought back to monoliteral terms by reference to the table at top of page 111. And the 3rd operation will give us:

2nd cipher : BA DB DA BC DD AB BA BE AA BD
3rd cryptogram : E O L T A A E B M R
2nd cipher : AC CA BC DC CB AD BB DA EC AE
3rd cryptogram : N D T P F C S L X H
2nd cipher BB AD
3rd cryptogram : S C

which will be transmitted as:

EOLTQ AEBMR NDTPF CSLXH SCZZZ

Mention must also be made of two simple ciphers of great antiquity—they are sometimes used to-day and are quite easy to decipher. They have provided a base for some of the more complicated modern ciphers.

The first of these is a transposition cipher—orderly mixing up of letters. Write the message up and down the columns in the Chinese manner, beginning on the right. The first column reads down, the second up, and so on.

Plain text, 'We have no food and must surrender.'

A	U	S	O	O	W
A	R ⁵	T	D ³	F	E ¹
R	R	S	A	O	H
E	E	U	N	N	A
D ⁶	N	M ⁴	D	E ²	V

↓

Cryptograms : AUSOOW ARTDFE RRSAOH EEUNNA DNMDEV

The other is a simple substitution cipher—a simplification of Porta's table:

Plain text : 'Meeting brigade village crossroads.'

Use for each word a different alphabet, preceding the

TYPES OF CODES AND CIPHERS 113

word with the indications, 'W', 'X', 'Y', or 'Z' as the case may be.

$W\begin{cases}A & B & C & D & E & F & G & H & IJ & K \\ L & M & N & O & P & R & S & T & V & X\end{cases}$

$X\begin{cases}K & IJ & H & G & F & E & D & C & B & A \\ L & M & N & O & P & R & S & T & W & Y\end{cases}$

$Y\begin{cases}A & C & E & G & IJ & L & N & P & S & W \\ B & D & F & H & K & M & O & R & T & Y\end{cases}$

$Z\begin{cases}A & B & C & D & E & L & M & N & O & P \\ F & G & H & IJ & K & R & S & T & W & Y\end{cases}$

Cryptogram : W BPPHWCS   X WEMOYSR   Y YKMMBHF
Z HLWMMLWFIM

3. *Numeral or Figure Ciphers*

In the most simple cases figure ciphers mean only that letters are replaced by numbers. Arbitrarily, the equivalent of A, B, C, D, etc., may stand for any numbers from 10 to 99, and without any over. The odd pairs of figures may represent either frequently-used syllables (as in Louis XIV and Napoleon's ciphers mentioned in Chapter II) or a complete code of short sentences or personal names (as in the Duke of Brandenburg's cipher, see Chapter II).

Another use for numbers is as keywords. Instead of 'Manchester' as keyword you can simply use the current dates, as for instance 2. 5. 1948, or any other sequence of numbers.

Again, certain figures—say from 100 to 999—can be used instead of words as a kind of dictionary code.

Selenus, Duke of Luneburg, gave a suggestion for the first numeral code. It is an interesting one, for instead of being alphabetical, it is composed of syllables. Here it is:

	1	2	3	4	5	6
1	AB	AH	AN	AG	AM	AT
2	EC	EK	EG	EF	EM	ES
3	ID	IE	IR	ID	IL	IW
4	OF	OM	OS	OC	OK	OG
5	UG	UN	UB	UT	UF	UP

H

He does not describe how it can be used; and as he only gives (a vowel) + (a consonant) and not (a consonant) + (a vowel), some words would be difficult to encipher; but it may serve as a foundation for a syllable cipher which may be quite interesting for the reader to compose.

4. *Dictionary Code Systems*

These are highly specialized forms of substitution systems, and involve the use of modified dictionaries known as code books. The commercial uses of these codes were explained in Chapter IV, but the code books used by the Foreign Office or for military purposes represent a greater condensation—a single code group may represent a long phrase. The average condensation of a diplomatic code is often 1:5 while in a commercial code it is only 1:3.

These groups, as we have seen, are all pronounceable artificial words, such as 'ABACA' for instance in a commercial code or 'EXA' in a Diplomatic code, and occasionally syllables such as 'BA', as we have seen in examples of Marconi codes.

As it is difficult to safeguard against the loss of code books, which have to be printed in great numbers, they do not afford such security as ciphers, although, of course, so long as they are kept secret, they are very good.

A story about a dictionary code is told by Mr. J. C. H. Macbeth. During the Russo-Turkish war in 1877, the Ottoman Field-Marshal Osman Pasha entrusted one of his generals, Selim Pasha, with a confidential mission. It so happened that Selim was the officer responsible for ciphering, and being prudent, he always kept the code on his person. Unfortunately, he departed so promptly on his

TYPES OF CODES AND CIPHERS

mission that he forgot to leave the volume with his chief. And the latter, during the whole time of his Adjutant's absence, saw a pile of ciphered telegrams from Constantinople accumulate on his table without being able to read or reply to them.

Codes, of course, can be used in conjunction with ciphers, and an enciphered code of this kind should be very difficult to break; but the work and time involved in making such a combination would be a serious objection. Speed of encoding and decoding is essential.

One of the ways in which ordinary dictionaries can be used is first to agree on a certain edition, say, for instance, the *Concise Oxford Dictionary*, current edition, by Fowler and Le Mesurier, and then to give only the number of the page, and the number of the word down the page. 'Reunion Berlin to-morrow' would be enciphered thus:

1006 (page no.) 12 (word no.) = Reunion.

0104 (pages with fewer than 4 numbers would have 'o' added in front to keep to the uniformity) 17 (word no.) = Berlin.

1291–08 (on the same principle) = To-morrow.

And the cryptogram would read:

'100612   010417   129108.'

These figures, if greater secrecy is required, could again be enciphered and thus converted into letters by means of an agreed cipher. For that purpose it would be better to arrange for the second operation. Divide the figures into pairs and then convert them into letters by means of the table given on p. 116.

CODES AND CIPHERS

2nd Figure

		1	3	5	2	4	9	7	8	6	0
	9	AN	DA	HN	JT	MB	KC	GF	ES	BZ	ZA
	2	CK	AO	DB	HO	JS	GE	ER	BY	FR	YB
	7	IR	CJ	AP	DC	GD	EQ	BT	FQ	LH	VA
1st figure	4	MC	IY	CI	AR	DD	BS	FP	LI	NL	VB
	8	MA	KB	GC	CG	AS	DF	HP	JU	OB	VC
	1	KA	GB	EP	BR	CE	AT	DG	HQ	JQ	TZ
	5	GA	EO	BP	FO	IX	CC	AX	DH	HR	TY
	3	EN	BO	FN	LJ	NK	IZ	CB	AY	DJ	SB
	6	BN	FM	LK	NJ	OA	OC	IV	CB	AZ	QA
	0	XY	YA	BY	YB	XC	XE	YD	YE	YX	QC

NULLS : WA, WE, W, to end message in groups of five letters.

The numbers enciphered into letters would be:
TZYXBR XYXCDG BRANYE
and the cryptogram for transmission would be:
TZYXB RXYXC DGBRA NYEWA

The suggested cipher can easily be arranged to make pronounceable words, suitable for telegraph transmission.

Certain dictionaries have been issued which give the two columns on each page with words directly opposite to each other. Then it is possible to give the word opposite the one we really mean, or a word which is 5 or 3 or 10 places either above or below the one we want to encode. Codes of this kind can be solved without difficulty, and I will give an example in the next chapter.

5. *Cryptographic Machines*

Professor Wheatstone was the first person to invent and patent a cryptographic machine in 1861, although the principle of such a mechanical device was first conceived by Thomas Jefferson.

To-day there are a number of these machines in use, and they vary in complexity from simple superimposed and rotating disks to large, mechanically, or even electrically-operated typewriting and telegraphic machines, but modified for cryptographic purposes.

The cylindrical apparatus invented by Bazeries in 1891 is of a simple mechanical type and consists of 20 disks bearing numbers 1-20. They are assembled on a common shaft from left to right according to a numerical key. In encipherment these disks are revolved so as to bring the plain text letters on a single horizontal line, and then the letters of any other horizontal line are taken as cipher equivalents. In deciphering the letters are set upon one horizontal line by revolving the disks and locking them into position. Then, when the whole cylinder is turned round slowly and each horizontal line is read, one of these will yield an intelligible text.

One of the latest pieces of telegraphic apparatus embodies a very complicated cipher machine. In this system electrical encipherment, transmission, reception, and decipherment can be accomplished almost simultaneously by means of perforated tapes. All these machines, however, even those with a typewriting keyboard, do not provide the degree of secrecy required for government use, and are therefore not used to any large extent.

6. *Syko*

The principal requirement of all codes and ciphers used in war is the speed of encoding and decoding, as well as a reasonable guarantee of immediate security against breaking. Obviously, if the breaking of the cipher takes too long, the operation covered by it will already have been carried out. It should be remembered that in the 1939-45 war, during the German blitz advance into the Low Countries, the German High Command dispensed with codes and ciphers, and gave all their orders to the forward troops in clear, relying on the

CODES AND CIPHERS

momentum and speed of the advance to make it impossible for counter measures to be taken. Their policy was successful.

An ingenious semi-mechanical kind of cipher machine,

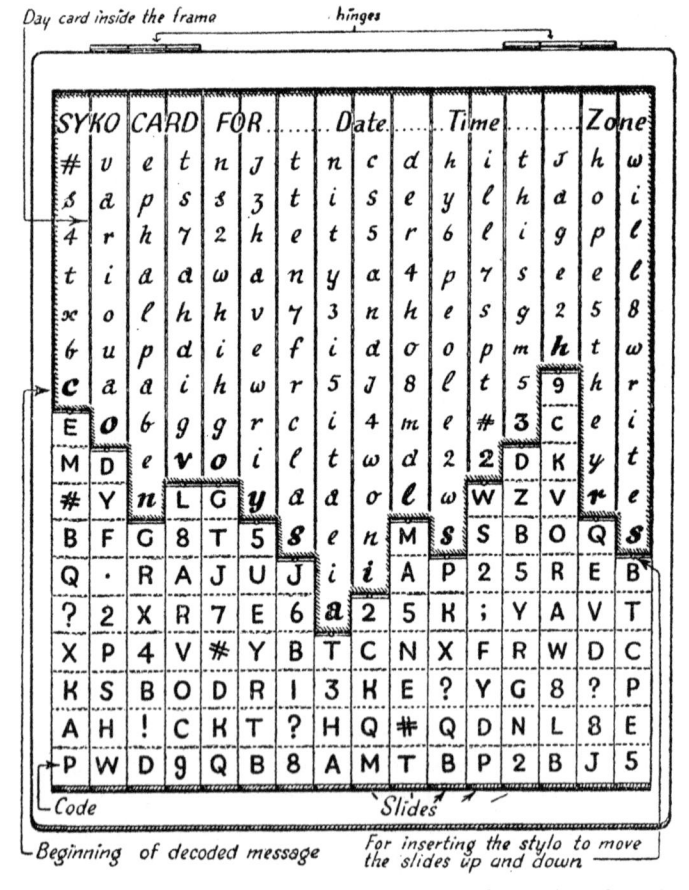

Day card inside the frame   *hinges*

SY	KO	CA	RD	FO	R		D	ate		Ti	me		Zo	ne
#	v	e	t	n	J	t	n	c	d	h	i	t	J	h	ω
s	d	p	s	s	3	t	i	s	e	y	l	h	d	o	i
4	r	h	7	2	h	e	t	5	r	6	l	i	g	p	l
t	i	d	d	ω	d	n	y	a	4	p	7	s	e	e	l
x	o	l	h	h	v	7	3	n	h	e	s	g	2	5	8
6	u	p	d	i	e	f	i	d	σ	o	p	m	h	t	ω
c	a	d	i	h	ω	r	5	J	8	l	t	5	9	h	r
E	o	6	g	g	r	c	i	4	m	e	#	3	C	e	i
M	D	e	v	o	i	l	t	ω	d	2	2	D	K	y	t
#	Y	n	L	G	y	a	d	σ	l	ω	W	Z	V	r	e
B	F	G	8	T	5	s	e	n	M	s	S	B	O	Q	s
Q	.	R	A	J	U	J	i	i	A	P	2	5	R	E	B
?	2	X	R	7	E	6	a	2	5	H	;	Y	A	V	T
X	P	4	V	#	Y	B	T	C	N	X	F	R	W	D	C
K	S	B	O	D	R	I	3	H	E	?	Y	G	8	?	P
A	H	!	C	K	T	?	H	Q	#	Q	D	N	L	8	E
P	W	D	9	Q	B	8	A	M	T	B	P	2	B	J	5

Code   *Slides*

Beginning of decoded message   *For inserting the stylo to move the slides up and down*

A diagrammatic sketch of a Syko frame with the day card inside. For clarity the number of vertical slides has been reduced to sixteen instead of thirty-two.

called the 'Syko', was invented during this war for carrying in aircraft. It was composed, first of all, of a hinged frame, on the front of which were 32 vertical slides bearing all the letters of the alphabet and a few signs, rather in the manner of Vigénère's table. Each of these slides could be moved vertically up and down the full length of the frame (about 10 or 12 inches).

A printed card bearing letters and symbols, a different one for every day of the month, was inserted into the frame so that, as the front slides were moved up and down by means of a stylo, each uncovered a vertical column of the day card, on which were printed scrambled letters and symbols.

To encode, the slides were moved in turn in a downward direction until the letter, figure or symbol which was needed came to rest along the bottom row of the frame. The characters showing on the day card immediately above the top of the slides provided the coded version. These were extracted in groups of four, reading from left to right. Decoding was carried out in reverse. The character in code was pulled down on the slide until it came to rest along the bottom row of the frame; the character on the day card immediately above the top edge of the slide was then taken as the decode.

The method of coding and decoding proved extremely useful, as it was moderately safe from breaking, could be used very quickly, and also took up very little room in the aircraft.

The coded message was 'PWD9oB8AMTBP2BJ5'; the slides were pulled up or down till these letters came at the bottom of the frame. The message was then revealed on the day card by reading the characters immediately above the slides: 'Convoy sails 23 hrs'.

7. Musical Code

In a typical code of this sort one minim stands for A, two for E, three for I, etc., and then 20 notes for the letter T, 10 chords for J, 16 for P, etc. They could be played or written so that they made a tune.

There was a code of this kind shown some years ago in an unusually good political-detective film called *The Lady Vanishes*.

Here is an example of a musical code:

Another variation of the same code can be made up by the five vowels expressed by single minims, and the letters by chords. With a little trill or previously arranged tune between, a message can be actually 'played' without any one being the wiser.

CHAPTER VII
METHODS OF DECIPHERING

THERE is a very sad story which shows that the lack of knowledge of the elementary deciphering principles may sometimes play an important role in one's life.

In 1674 the Chevalier de Rohan, a French general, was accused of having abandoned Quilleboeuf, a small French fortress, to the Dutch. He and his chief counsellor, La Truaumont, were arrested and taken to the Bastille. La Truaumont on the way there escaped, and after a long chase was killed by the guards. De Rohan, who had been shut in the Bastille, did not know what had happened, nor whether he had been betrayed.

De Rohan's friends tried to inform him of the state of affairs so that he could save himself from the gallows by denying his complicity in the plot. Amongst his clean laundry they smuggled in a shirt on which was written the following cryptogram:

MG EULHXCCLGU GHJ YXUJ; LM CT ULGC ALJ.

The prisoner could not decipher this, although naturally he tried very hard, and later, when cross-examined at the trial, he admitted his guilt and was beheaded.

If he had only known any of the principles of cryptography he would have solved this cipher without any difficulty.

Three letters, C, G and H are repeated four times, so one of them is presumably E. In French the trigram 'est' is the most common; therefore presumably GHJ = est.

The bigram MG can be read as 'je' or 'le'. If we try 'le', then the fifth group may well be 'il', another common bigram in French. We will now fill in the letters we know so far:

Cipher :   MG DULHXCCLGU GHJ YXUJ LM CT
Plain text :   le   i s   i e   e s t   t   i l

Cipher :   ULGC ALJ
Plain text :   i e   i t

Now consider the fourth group. We have the last letter, 't', and two possible French words of four letters ending in 't' come to mind, 'fort' and 'mort'; let us try the second.

The seventh group ULGC can now be partly filled in: 'rie–'; this must surely be 'rien'.

It is now clear that the message reads:

'Le prisonier est mort—il n'a rien dit.' ('The prisoner is dead ; he has said nothing.')

Although concentration and perseverance may go a long way towards enabling us to solve complicated cryptograms without a key, yet we are not likely to be very successful until we have acquired some practical knowledge and experience of the art.

I propose, therefore, to give some hints on the procedure to be adopted when trying to decipher. At the same time I cannot promise that these hints by themselves will enable any one to become an expert decipherer. However, it may be amusing, if nothing else, to try to follow the examples given below of the *modus operandi*. The would-be decipherer had better first arm himself with one or two manuals of cryptography which give the frequency tables, one or two dictionaries, a rhyming dictionary, some squared paper, tracing paper, a graduated ruler, and even perhaps a T-square (for the Vigénère table). Counters on which the letters of the alphabet are printed are often more efficient than writing out the whole cryptogram, as one letter at a time can easily be altered. Finally, coloured pencils make the whole thing easier.

You must be orderly and systematic; nothing is more likely to hinder you in deciphering than bits of paper and scrawls all over the cryptogram. If you keep a systematic filing of your cipher as you go along you will help yourself very considerably.

The first thing to do is to find out whether the cryptogram is in code or in cipher. An expert will generally be able to decide that entirely by its external appearance. If it is a cipher you must then dicover whether it is a transposition or substitution. This is deduced from the fact that, in plain text, vowels and consonants are present in definite proportions. Transposition involves a rearrangement of the original letters, and if the proportion of vowels to consonants seems more or less than approximately normal, we may conclude that the cryptogram belongs to the transposition class. If not, then to a substitution system.

Deciphering of Substitution Systems

To be quite frivolous for a moment, if we had to encipher 'the dog is bad' by substitution, we could put 'z' for 'a', 'y' for 'b', 'x' for 'c', etc.; whereas using transposition the same sentence could read 'EHT GOD SI DAB', in this case the letters being simply reversed.

The solution of transposition ciphers involves a series of experiments with geometrical designs of various types and dimensions, clues to which can be looked for in the number of letters in the message and other circumstances; e.g., pairs of letters present in great numbers may give a hint of their values.

The frequency with which certain letters appear in certain languages is well known. I have already referred to this when describing the principles of Morse code (p. 73).

Frequency Tables

Various tables show slight differences in the actual order of letter frequencies. This depends of course on the kind of book taken in order to count the frequencies. Edgar Allan Poe for instance used one of his own books, Morse used the Bible, the telegraph frequencies were taken at random from actual telegrams. "Normal" frequency was calculated in America. It is rather amusing in the circumstances that there is not a greater divergence in the order of letters used. But E, T. O, and A certainly seem to be used more frequently than others.

In English, a count of 100,000 gives the following relative frequencies in 1,000 letters:

E	T	R	I	N	O	A	S	D	L	C	H	F	U
126	90	83	76	76	74	72	58	40	36	33	33	30	30

P	M	Y	G	W	V	B	X	K	Q	J	Z
27	25	21	18	14	13	11	5	3	3	2	1

Other frequency tables are:

Edgar Allan Poe : E A O I D H N R S T U Y

Kerckhoff : E T A O N I R S H D L C W U M

Vesin de Romanini : E T I O N A S H

Thomas : E T A I S O N H R D L U C M F W Y P G B V K J Q X Z.

Normal frequencies : E T O A N I R S H D L U C M P F Y W G B V K J X Z Q.

Telegraph frequencies : E O A N I R S T D L H U C M P Y F G W B V K X J Q Z.

Valerio (per 1,000 letters) :

E	T	O	A	N	I	R	S	H	D
131	90	82	78	73	68	67	65	59	41

L	C	F	U	M	P	Y	W	G	B	V	K	X	J	Q	Z
36	29	28	28	26	22	15	15	14	13	10	4	3	1	1	1

METHODS OF DECIPHERING

Valerio has also computed the frequency with which letters occur at the ends of words, and gives the following table per 1,000 letters.

E	S	D	N	T	R	Y	O	F	A	G	L	H	I	M	W
66	41	40	32	32	28	27	17	10	9	9	9	8	8	7	2

K	U C X
2	1

J, Q, V, Z are not met with.

Mansfield : E T S D Y G N R M H C P, etc.

If the cipher is a simple mono-alphabetic substitution, then using the frequency tables above will help us to solve it. Supposing we were handed, for deciphering, the following message:

KRBRYMT DYQRYRQ ZJR WRPDBQ NYIKMQR ZD MZZMPO MZ ZJYRR ZJIYZG MU ZJR ZJIYQ NYIKMQR DBR JDAY TMZRY DB ZJR TRSZ ZJR SDAYZJ ZD ORRH IB YRWRYCR.

(For simplicity we have not broken up the cryptogram into five-letter groups.)

Now we will prepare an analytical table of this cipher thus:

A	....	2	N	....	2
B	....	5	O	....	2
C	....	1	P	....	2
D	....	8	Q	....	6
E	....		R	....	21
F	....		S	....	2
G	....	1	T	....	3
H	....	1	U	....	3
I	....	4	V	....	
J	....	8	W	....	2
K	....	3	X	....	
L	....		Y	....	13
M	....	8	Z	....	16

126   CODES AND CIPHERS

The examination of the analysis table shows that the letters occurring most often are:

R	Z	Y	D	J	M
21	16	13	8	8	8

We do not need to go any farther, for if we establish even a few of these letters, no doubt we shall be able to solve the cryptogram.

Looking up Thomas's table of frequencies and supposing the cryptogram is in English, we find that 'E' is the most commonly used letter and 'T' the second. This enables us to take the value of 'R' as 'E' and the value of 'Z' as 'T'. We write these letters over the corresponding letters in the cryptogram, to each group of which we also give a number. We cannot yet write the others as the cryptogram is too short to allow for the law of averages to operate (with the exception of 'E' and 'T'). Again this can be simplified by using counters instead of actually writing it all down.

Plain text:	E E		E E	T E	E	
Cipher:	KRBRYMT	DYQRYRQ		ZJR	WRPDBQ	
Group:	1	2		3	4	

Plain text:		E	T	TT	T	T EE
Cipher:	NYIKMQR	ZD		MZZMPO	MZ	ZJYRR
Group:	5	6		7	8	9

Plain text:	T T		T E	T		E
Cipher:	ZJIYZG	MU	ZJR	ZJIYQ	NYIKMQR	
Group:	10	11	12	13	14	

Plain text:	E		T E		T E	E T	T E
Cipher:	DBR	JDAY	TMZRY	DB	ZJR	TRSZ	ZJR
Group:	15	16	17	18	19	20	21

Plain text:	T T		EE		E E	E	
Cipher:	SDAYZJ	ZD	ORRH	IB	YRWRYCR		
Group:	22	23	24	25	26		

Let us now consider the two-letter groups; we have six of them:

Table of 2-letter groups

6th	8th	11th	18th	23rd	25th
T	T			T	
ZD	MZ	MU	DB	ZD	IB

We know that 'Z' is equivalent to 'T' so we mark those on the top.

We have these frequencies for two-letter words (Valerio): 'of, to, in, it, or, is, be, he, by, or, as, at, an, so.' We observe that the letter 'T' occurs in 'To' (as first letter) and 'iT' and 'aT' (as second letter). 'ZD' occurs twice and we can therefore take it to mean 'To'. 'D' in the cipher we now take as equivalent to 'O' and we mark the cipher accordingly.

The commonest bigrams are as follows:
TH HE AN ER ON RE IN ED ND AT OF OR HA EN NT EA.

We observe the recurrence of 'ZJ' in our cryptogram in the 3rd, 9th, 10th, 12th, 13th, 19th, 21st, and 22nd groups. The significance of this is even more striking when we consider the three-letter words. 'ZJR' occurs four times in the 3rd, 12th, 19th, and 21st groups. We know the value of Z = T and R = E, and as the commonest trigram is 'THE', we conclude that J = H. The following is the table of common trigrams: the, and, tha, hat, edt (tried to, carried the) cut, for ion, tio, nde, has, men, nce, oft, sth.

Now let us see how the cryptogram looks with all the so far known plain text letters written above the others—this time using our coloured chalks.

R = E, Z = T, D = O, J = H

Plain text:	E E	O E E	THE	E O	
Cipher:	KRBRYMT	DYQRYRQ	ZJR	WRPDBQ	
Plain text:	E	TO	TT	T	TH EE
Cipher:	NYIKMQR	ZD	MZZMPO	MZ	ZJYRR

128   CODES AND CIPHERS

Plain text :	TH	T		THE	TH		E
Cipher :	ZJIYZG	MU		ZJR	ZJIYQ		NYIKMQR
Plain text :	O E		HO	E	O	THE	E T
Cipher :	DBR		JDAY	TMZRY	DB	ZJR	TRSZ
Plain text :	THE	O	TH	TO	EE		E E E
Cipher :	ZJR	SDAYZJ	ZD	ORRH	IB		YRWRYCR

We then look at it carefully, rather in the way we fill in the easy words of a crossword puzzle. We at once notice that the ninth group: 'TH-EE' is most probably 'THREE' and we decide that 'Y' = 'R', which we write in.

The 15th group: 'DBR' = 'O-E' we try as 'ONE', and we conclude 'B' = 'N'. We now rewrite the plain text leaving blanks for unknown letters:

- ENER - - OR - ERE - THE - E - ON - - R - - - - E TO
- TT - - - - T THREE TH - RT - - - THE TH - R - - R - - - - E
ONE HO - R - - - ER ON THE - E - T THE - - - RTH TO
- EE - - N RE - ER - E

The word 'TH-RT-', looks like 'thirty', giving us cipher 'I' equal to plain text 'I', and cipher 'G' = 'Y'. The '-T' preceding 'three thirty' is almost certainly 'at', giving us cipher 'M' = 'A', and 'HO-R' must be 'hour', which makes cipher 'A' = 'U'.

How does our cryptogram look now?

- ENERA - OR - ERE - THE - E - ON - - RI - A - E TO
ATTA - - AT THREE THIRTY A - THE THIR - - RI - A - E
ONE HOUR - ATER ON THE - E - T THE - OURTH - EE -
IN RE - ER - E.

I now suggest that an interested reader should arm himself with a paper and pencil and finish off the deciphering. I would advise him not to mark the book, as some one else reading it may like to try his hand as well. I give the solution at the end of this chapter.

METHODS OF DECIPHERING

I asked a friend to give me a cryptogram to decipher without letting me know anything about the kind of cipher that was used. As I think it was quite instructive from the point of view of the mistakes I made, and the mistakes made also by my friend in taking the cipher down, I shall give it here. This is what I received:

CDD BCECBCE BBEBDAB CCBBD BAB CCDCDBCD DEC AECB
DDDAA CABCE AABD EBCEDCBCCD AEBDCB AAEA BECDDB
DCCEC EEABDA DEADCA ADEACABDCBDCBA ABDCACEDC
BABCDD CDBDDC BEBCDC BEBCAA BDACCDDBBBCEAACD
BDCDDBCEDCAECACEDC

It will be noticed at once that only the first five letters of the alphabet repeat themselves: 'ABCDE'. By certain repetitions, etc., in the crypt I felt, rather than was able to prove, that it was a two-letter cipher.

This is the principle of such a cipher:

		2nd letter			
	A	B	C	D	E
A	A	b	c	d	e
B	f	g	h	ij	k
C	l	m	n	o	p
D	q	r	s	t	u
E	v	w	x	y	z

1st letter

Example: ENEMY would be: AE for 'E', CC for 'N,' etc., making complete crypt: AE, CC, AE, CB, ED.

The letters are seldom put in such a straightforward alphabetical order; both the plain text and the cipher letters (capitals) would be all jumbled together and not put in any obvious order. In any case, the first procedure was to

I

separate the crypt in two-letter groups with red pencil, and then make up a frequency table, thus:

AA occurs 6 times	BA occurs twice	CA occurs twice
AB occurs twice	BB occurs twice	CB occurs 5 times
AC occurs 3 times	BC occurs 7 times	CC occurs 0 times
AD occurs once	BD occurs 9 times	CD occurs 9 times
AE occurs 3 times	BE occurs 3 times	CE occurs 10 times
DA occurs twice	EA occurs 3 times	
DB occurs 4 times	EB occurs twice	
DC occurs 9 times	EC occurs once	
DD occurs 3 times	ED occurs 0 times	
DE occurs once	EE occurs 0 times	

According to the table of frequencies, the group CE must be equivalent to the plain text 'E'. So we write it above the crypt in red pencil in appropriate places, this way:

```
         E           E
CD  DB  CE  CB   CE  BB  EB  DA  BC  CB  BD
___  ___
BA  BC  CD  CD   BC  DD  EC  AE  CB  DD  DA
         E                E
AC  AB  CE  AA   BD  EB  CE  DC  BC  CD  AE
                                   E    E
BD  CB  AA  EA   BE  CD  DB  DC  CE  CE  EA
                     ___  ___
BD  AD  EA  DC   AA  DE  AC  AB  DC  BD  CB
             E
AA  BD  CA  CE   DC  BA  BC  DD  CD  BD  DC

BE  BC  DC  BE   BC  AA  BD  AC  CD  DB  BB
 E                        E                E
CE  AA  CD  BD   CD  DB  CE  DC  AE  CA  CE
                 ___  ___
DC
```

On examining the crypt now we observe the repetition of the 'CD, DB' four times. This bigram forms on two

METHODS OF DECIPHERING 131

occasions part of the trigram CD, DB, CE, and the last group CE we know to be 'E'. The commonest bigram is 'th' and the most used trigram is 'the', so it is quite easy to deduce that 'CD, DB' stand for 'th'. Now take a red pencil and mark 'th' over the crypt yourself.

It was here that I went wrong. I looked at the line before last of this group

    AA BD AC CD DB BB CE AA CD

Fitting in the letters we know, it looks like this:

    AA, BD, AC, th, BB, e AA t,

and I jumped to the conclusion that it was 'North West'. The group BD occurs nine times, and the table of frequencies gives us 'O' as being very near to 'E' in recurrence; but 'AA' stood in the beginning for 'N' in 'north' and for 'S' in 'west', and that did not fit. But 'South West' would fit very well in all cases.

So I started to mark the appropriate letters in the cipher with the plain text letters thus derived, when I observed the following group on the fourth line:

    CD DB DC CE CE

or if I put in the values which have been already deduced—'t, h, DC, e,e'. There is only one word of five letters 'TH?EE' and this is 'three'. So we have one more letter to add to the plain text—'R'.

So let us see once more how the crypt reads now, when we fill in the plain text values we know.

AA = S   CE = E   AC = U   DC = R
CD = T   BB = W   BD = O   DB = H

The - CB, e, w, EB, DA, BC, CB, o, BA, BC, t, t, BC, DD, EC, AE, CB, DD, DA, u, AB, e, s, o, EB, e, r, BC, t, AE, o, CB, s, EA, BE,—three—EA, o, AD, EA, r, s, DE, u, AB, r, o, CB, s, o, CA, e, r, BA, BC, DD, t, o, r, BE, BC, r, BE , BC, - south - west - o, the, r, AE, CA, e, r.

My attention was drawn next to the following groups: 'o, CA, e, r,' and the last group: 'r, AE, CA, e, r.' If the first be taken as 'over' then the value of CA = V, in second group we have 'rAEver' which was 'river' and that did moreover make sense; '... south west of the river' and here I come to the first mistake made by the 'encipherer'. The 'F' was omitted from the word 'of'.

This made me realize that probably other omissions would be met with in the crypt; but in any case we had two more letters to add to our plain text values: CA = v and AE = i.

Now once again take a red pencil and mark over the cryptogram AE = i, as there are no more 'CA' groups to mark. At once this group 'o,EB,e,r,BC,t,i,o,CB,s' jumps to the eye. If we write it this way 'o?er?tio?s'—it can only be 'operations'. This will give us the values of E B = p, BC = a, CB = n.

If we write these new values in, the crypt will now look as follows:

The new p (DA) an o(BA) atta(DD) (EC) in (DD) (DA) u(AB)es operations (EA) (BE) three (EA)o (AD) (EA) rs (DE) u (AB)rons over (BA) a(DD)tor (BE) ar(BE) a south west o? the river.

The group 'atta(DD) (EC)' can only mean 'attack' or 'attacking', but the value of 'DD' being 'C' in this case, it precludes 'attacking', and the following word 'inc(DA)u (AB)es' looks like 'includes'.

The new plan o(BA) attack includes operations (EA) (BE) three (EA)o(AD) (EA) r s (DE) (drons over (BA)actor(BE)ar(BE)a south west o? the river.

'plan o(BA) attack' gives the only possible value to 'BA = f', and 'operations (EA) (BE) three ...' must be read as 'EA,BE = by'.

Now if you bear in mind that we have already found one

METHODS OF DECIPHERING 133

mistake in ' . . . south west o? the river'—'f' in the 'of' missing—you must be prepared for other mistakes. There are two missing letters and one misspelling; nevertheless, if the last three values found are written in, the sense of the message is apparent.

It is very common in deciphering to come across mistakes either by the encipherer or by telegraphists, signallers, or others concerned with the transmission of the cipher. If the above example had been without errors the deciphering would have been easier, but even as it was we succeeded in getting the sense completely.

Vigénère Ciphers (Poly-alphabetic System)

I shall now try to show the way to tackle a cipher which has been enciphered by means of a compound alphabet key.

Let us examine this cryptogram:

1	2	3	4	5
PWRPM	KGZHJ	IVFMF	KXKGZ	HFBKG
6	7	8	9	10
BKTMH	NIWGA	WFMVR	IWEPH	UXOGI
11	12	13	14	15
VGLLU	KRPBL	PCHVP	HUMFK	XKGZV
16	17	18	19	20
CAWJM	RPMVW	AHFPL	VPHTB	RYMUG
21				
JHVBH				

At first sight it seems a hopeless job when we realize that there were three, five, or eight alphabets used to encipher this cryptogram. The solution looks well-nigh impossible.

Yet when anything is reduced to a science there is a method, so that at least an approach can be made to start with. We shall first of all note the repetitions such as 'RPM' in the first and 17th group, and underline them. Let us count the spaces that separate similar repetitions:

	RPM to R'P'M'— 78 spaces =	26 × 3
(2nd group	KGZ to K'G'Z'— 12 spaces =	4 × 3
to 4th)	PH to P'H' — 21 spaces =	7 × 3
	VPH to V'P'H'— 27 spaces =	9 × 3

There is no need to count any further—we can now safely assume that the key is a word of three letters as three is the only common denominator. So let us put the crypt in a three-letter order like this:

PWR	PMK	GZH	JIV	FMF	KXK	GZH	FBK
GBK	TMH	NIW	GAW	FMV	RIW	EPH	UXO
GIV	GLL	UKR	PBL	PCH	VPH	UMF	KXK
GZV	CAW	JMR	PMV	WAH	FPL	VPH	TBR
YMU	GJH	VBH					

In a poly-alphabetic crypt it is usual for all the first letters of these three-letter groups to belong to the first alphabet, the middle letters to the second, and the end letters to the third, so we draw another table.

1st Alphabet	2nd Alphabet	3rd Alphabet
FFFF	W	RRRR
PPPPP	MMMMMMMM	KKKKK
GGGGGGGG	ZZZ	HHHHHHHHHH
JJ	IIII	VVVVV
KK	XXX	FF
TT	BBBBB	WWWW
N	AAA	O
R	PPPP	LLL
E	L	U
UUU	K	
VVV	C	
C	J	
W		
Y		

We can see at once that the letters 'G' in the 1st alphabet, 'M' in the 2nd, and 'H' in the 3rd stand in each case for 'E', and by reference to Vigénère's table we find that the 'E's' are denoted in the first case by 'C' alphabet, in the second by the 'I' alphabet, and in the third by 'D'. That gives us the key word 'CID', and we can now decipher the rest. The complete answer is given at the end of this chapter.

Invented Alphabets

It will be clear that the rules of frequencies will be applicable to invented alphabets as well. Signs as well as numerals can be used for substitution systems, and if a certain sign repeats itself sufficiently often it will always mean 'E'. The same general principles will apply to the bigram 'th' and the trigram 'the', etc., as have been described above. I shall not give an example of this kind of cipher, but let the reader make up one for himself, for instance, on Charlemagne's type, or one like the Freemasons', and see if he can decipher it without having the alphabet handy a day or two later, when the signs will be forgotten.

Deciphering of Transposition Systems

The examples given above all belong to substitution systems, and we now turn our attention to the transposition ciphers.

I have mentioned in Chapter I the very old method of the 'skytale', used by the Spartans in Greece. All transposition ciphers are actually based on this method, but instead of writing lines of letters on strips of paper and winding them round a rod, we simply transpose the letters in vertical columns, using a keyword or the equivalent in numerical sequence (see p. 104 in Chapter VI).

CODES AND CIPHERS

	A	B	C	D	E	F	G	H	I	J	K	L	M
A	a	b	c	d	e	f	g	h	i	j	k	l	m
B	b	c	d	e	f	g	h	i	j	k	l	m	n
C	c	d	e	f	g	h	i	j	k	l	m	n	o
D	d	e	f	g	h	i	j	k	l	m	n	o	p
E	e	f	g	h	i	j	k	l	m	n	o	p	q
F	f	g	h	i	j	k	l	m	n	o	p	q	r
G	g	h	i	j	k	l	m	n	o	p	q	r	s
H	h	i	j	k	l	m	n	o	p	q	r	s	t
I	i	j	k	l	m	n	o	p	q	r	s	t	u
J	j	k	l	m	n	o	p	q	r	s	t	u	v
K	k	l	m	n	o	p	q	r	s	t	u	v	w
L	l	m	n	o	p	q	r	s	t	u	v	w	x
M	m	n	o	p	q	r	s	t	u	v	w	x	y
N	n	o	p	q	r	s	t	u	v	w	x	y	z
O	o	p	q	r	s	t	u	v	w	x	y	z	a
P	p	q	r	s	t	u	v	w	x	y	z	a	b
Q	q	r	s	t	u	v	w	x	y	z	a	b	c
R	r	s	t	u	v	w	x	y	z	a	b	c	d
S	s	t	u	v	w	x	y	z	a	b	c	d	e
T	t	u	v	w	x	y	z	a	b	c	d	e	f
U	u	v	w	x	y	z	a	b	c	d	e	f	g
V	v	w	x	y	z	a	b	c	d	e	f	g	h
W	w	x	y	z	a	b	c	d	e	f	g	h	i
X	x	y	z	a	b	c	d	e	f	g	h	i	j
Y	y	z	a	b	c	d	e	f	g	h	i	j	k
Z	z	a	b	c	d	e	f	g	h	i	j	k	l
	A	B	C	D	E	F	G	H	I	J	K	L	M

Modified Vigénère Table

METHODS OF DECIPHERING

N	O	P	Q	R	S	T	U	V	W	X	Y	Z	
n	o	p	q	r	s	t	u	v	w	x	y	z	A
o	p	q	r	s	t	u	v	w	x	y	z	a	B
p	q	r	s	t	u	v	w	x	y	z	a	b	C
q	r	s	t	u	v	w	x	y	z	a	b	c	D
r	s	t	u	v	w	x	y	z	a	b	c	d	E
s	t	u	v	w	x	y	z	a	b	c	d	e	F
t	u	v	w	x	y	z	a	b	c	d	e	f	G
u	v	w	x	y	z	a	b	c	d	e	f	g	H
v	w	x	y	z	a	b	c	d	e	f	g	h	I
w	x	y	z	a	b	c	d	e	f	g	h	i	J
x	y	z	a	b	c	d	e	f	g	h	i	j	K
y	z	a	b	c	d	e	f	g	h	i	j	k	L
z	a	b	c	d	e	f	g	h	i	j	k	l	M
a	b	c	d	e	f	g	h	i	j	k	l	m	N
b	c	d	e	f	g	h	i	j	k	l	m	n	O
c	d	e	f	g	h	i	j	k	l	m	n	o	P
d	e	f	g	h	i	j	k	l	m	n	o	p	Q
e	f	g	h	i	j	k	l	m	n	o	p	q	R
f	g	h	i	j	k	l	m	n	o	p	q	r	S
g	h	i	j	k	l	m	n	o	p	q	r	s	T
h	i	j	k	l	m	n	o	p	q	r	s	t	U
i	j	k	l	m	n	o	p	q	r	s	t	u	V
j	k	l	m	n	o	p	q	r	s	t	u	v	W
k	l	m	n	o	p	q	r	s	t	u	v	w	X
l	m	n	o	p	q	r	s	t	u	v	w	x	Y
m	n	o	p	q	r	s	t	u	v	w	x	y	Z
N	O	P	Q	R	S	T	U	V	W	X	Y	Z	

Modified Vigénère Table (*contd.*)

Sometimes it is a very tedious business to decipher such crypts. But there are some general rules, which, if followed, make it easier. For instance, suppose we have to solve the following:

EBYETTTREAOSHTOPPOHDRKRIITTNONTATUHI

One of the ways in which we could tackle this would be to try it for a simple transposition.

First of all we count the number of letters in the crypt; there are 36, which is 6 × 6, and we therefore construct a square accordingly,

E	T	H	H	I	T
B	R	T	D	T	A
Y	E	O	R	T	T
E	A	P	K	N	U
T	O	P	R	O	H
T	S	O	I	N	I

in which we write the cipher downwards in columns, remembering that transpositions are usually written this way.

Now we know that the plain text was written across the square and that the cipher was taken downwards. In this square we have the down columns obviously in the wrong order, and we must try to make out, if possible, one word, reading it across the square.

Let us consider the first line: 'ETHHIT'. We know that the letter 'T' is frequently followed by 'H' and that the commonest trigram is 'the'. These six letters of the crypt suggest at once that two 'th' bigrams are included in that one line, and one trigram 'the', but the question is which 'T' is to be coupled with which 'H'. This can only be solved by trial and error. Let us decide that the order of the columns is to be 3 1 2 5 6 4 and number them accordingly. The new square which we construct will be:

```
T H E T H I
R T B A D T
E O Y T R T
A P E U K N
O P T H R O
S O T I I N
```

We shall easily see that we used the correct 'T' for the first letter because presumably the first two words are 'the third . . .' and the second line starts with an 'R'. On the other hand, the second column with 'H' on top and 'TOPPO' under the 'H' is wrong, as the 'R' on the second line should be followed by 'D'. Apparently we chose the wrong 'H' column; the other one gives us on the second line 'D' after 'R' completing the word 'third'.

If we rearrange the column thus:

```
T H E T H I
R D B A T T
E R Y T O T
A K E U P N
O R T H P O
S I T I O N
```

the message at once assumes a comprehensible form.

Actually the transposition systems are more difficult to solve than substitution because it takes a great deal of patience and perseverance to plod through dozens of possible combinations of letters before we get the right one; but, on the other hand, the satisfaction derived when the message at last can be read correctly is proportionately greater.

Dictionary Codes

I have already described the dictionary code, and it is clear that it would be the most difficult one to decipher. Yet Mr. Mansfield, an Australian criminologist of repute, has suggested some extremely interesting principles for the solving of such codes, and has even calculated dictionary progressive lists, giving numbers of words beginning with any two letters in dictionaries of 10, 20, 30, 40, 50, 60, 80, and 100 thousand words.

Mansfield's methods are very simple and ingenious. They are better demonstrated by an actual example. Let us take the case where all the words in a certain dictionary are numbered, and these numbers are transmitted as a code. Here is a message:

55381 42872 35284 55381 45174 56037 55381 46882
23171 44234 55366 55381 00723 12050 61571 36173
55381 56442

Let us analyse this list, starting from the lowest numbers and finishing with the highest.

00723	42872	55381 (5 times)
12050	44234	56037
23171	45174	56442
35284	46882	61571
36173	55366	

Words beginning with XYZ are seldom used, so we can take it that the highest number indicates a word beginning with a 'W' or a 'T'. But the list of frequencies gives us the commonest initial group as 'th' or 'the', and if we can find any repetition of such nature, that will fix 'T' in the dictionary. The group 55381 occurs five times in the crypt, so most probably it is 'the'.

METHODS OF DECIPHERING

The highest number after that is 61571, so that it should indicate a word beginning with a 'W.' This gives us the clue to the probable number of words in the dictionary used for that code. It cannot be over 65,000 as XYZ words are very few, seldom over 3000. Even in the largest dictionaries 60,000—65,000 words are quite common.

According to Mr. Mansfield's *Progressive Dictionary* we can now fix the probable first two letters of every word in the code. For instance, the second group 12050 will be between 11646 (terminating words beginning with 'DA') and 12850 (terminating those beginning with DE), so that it is certain to be a word beginning with DE. Using Mansfield's table we obtain:

'The re– of the ro– to– the se– – ha– re– th– the re– de– – wa– ov– the to–'

Now we can find in the dictionary the word 'the' (55381). We count back about twenty words for 55366 (th). This gives us an area covering the words 'thane', 'thank', 'that', 'thatch'. We will try 'that' as the most likely out of these. We now consider the groups 56037 and 56442. Words beginning with 'to' start at 56037 and stop at 56466, so that we should be justified in assuming the first to be 'to', while for the second (56442) we count back from the end of the 'to' section and find that 'town' seems the most likely word.

Let us now consider the 'r' group, 42872, 44234, and 45174. The 'Re's' begin at 42574 according to Mansfield's table, and counting 300 words from here gives us the following group to select from: 'recline', 'recommend', 'recompose', 'reconnaissance', 'recoup', and 'recover', and the word we choose is '*reconnaissance*'.

The same process brings us 'revealed' and 'route' for the other two.

What does the cipher look like with these few words put in?

> The reconnaissance of– the route to the se– ha– revealed that the ae– de– wa– ov– the town.

We apply the same process to 'ae–' 00723, and we get straight on to 'aeroplane', while 'de–' 12050 occurring one-quarter of the way from the end of DA to the end of DE brings us to DEF, limited by 'deface' and 'defy', where only 'defeat', 'defence', 'defend', and 'defensive' are probable. We can select 'aeroplane defensive' as near our mark.

The same process brings us 'sea' for 'se–' (46882) and 'over' for 'ov–' 36173. The complete message reads now:

> The reconnaissance 'of–' the route to the sea ha– revealed that the aeroplane(s) defensive wa– over the town.

We can easily see that 'of–' is merely 'of', 'ha–' is 'has', and 'wa–' is 'was'. The actual message differed only in two words: instead of 'aeroplanes' defensive' it was 'aerial defence', but the meaning was the same.

This application of the law of probability to dictionary codes is very interesting. The search in the area of possible words will at any rate give us the root of the plain text used in the actual code, and from that root we can usually deduce the whole of the meaning hidden by the code. (See Louis C. S. Mansfield: *The Solution of Codes and Ciphers*.)

The following lists may be of some use for deciphering purposes.

English diphthongs : ae, ai, ao, au, aw, ay, ea, ee, ei, eo, eu, ew, ey, ia, ie, oa, oe, oo, ou, ow, ue, ui.

Triphthongs : eau, eou, ieu, iew, iou.

Double consonants : ss, tt, ll, mm, ff, bb, cc, dd, gg, nn, pp, rr, zz.

METHODS OF DECIPHERING

Letters used most : E, T, I, O, N, A, S, H. But only the frequency of E can be relied upon.

Letters used least : Z, Q, J, X, K, Y.

Words terminating in : T, N, S, Y, D, E, especially E.

E and O are the easiest to discover, E because it is most often used, and O because it is the oftenest used as part of a bigram; also because both E and O are about the only ones used doubled in the middle of words of four letters.

Monograms : A, I, and sometimes O.

Bigrams : ab, ah, ad, at, an ; be, he, me, we, ge ; if, in, is, it ; do, go, lo, no, of, on, or, so, to, wo ; up, us, ut ; by, my, fy, ye.

Of these the order of frequency is: of and to, it, is, in, we, he, as, or, be, by, so and on.

If the first letter of a bigram is O, the second letter is usually F, N, or R.

If the first is T or S, the second is O.

If it is I, the second letter must be T, S, N, or F.

If it is W, H, or Y, the second is always E.

If the first is B, the second is E or Y.

If it is A, the second must be S, B, H, or T; most often S.

If two bigrams follow each other they will be TO DO, or DO NO.

If the first bigram is the same as the last of three bigrams, they will be TO DO TO, or TO GO TO.

If the first letters of two bigrams are the same, they will be IF IT, IN IT, IT IN, IT IS, OR OF, OR ON, but the first letters will always be either I or O.

If the first letter of the first bigram is equal to the second letter of the second bigram, it will be OF SO, OF TO, TO IT.

If the second letter of the first bigram equals the first letter of the second it will be AS SO, IS SO.

If we find a word which has this ending: ... 3166 × 166, we can at once decide that the second double letters are SS, the first two LE, and that the two preceding the second lot of double letters are NE, such as in 'blamelessness', 'dreadfulness', 'needlessness'.

Trigrams : THE, AND, THA, HET, EDT, ENT, FOR, ION, TIO, NDE, HAS, MEN, NCE, OFT, STH.

Three-letter words : THE, AND, FOR, ARE, NOT, BUT, HAD, HAS, YOU, WAS, HIS.

Four-letter words : THAT, WITH, HAVE, FROM, THEY, THEM, THIS, WHEN, WILL, OVER, BOTH.

Solution of crypt, p. 128 (mono-alphabetic substitution):

General ordered the second brigade to attack at 3.30 a.m. the third brigade one hour later on the left, the fourth keep in reserve.

Solution of Vigénère cipher, p. 135 (keyword CID):

No one here has deciphered the three latest dispatches, please discontinue these ciphers as the ones used hitherto were better.

Here is a cryptogram upon which the reader is invited to test his skill.

75628 28591 62916 48164 91748 58464 74748 28483 81638 18174
74826 26475 83828 49175 74658 37575 75936 36565 81638 17585
75756 46282 92857 46382 75748 38165 81848 56485 64858 56382
72628 36281 81728 16463 75828 16483 63828 58163 63630 47481
91918 46385 84656 48565 62946 26285 91859 17491 72756 46575
71658 36264 74818 28462 82649 18193 65626 48484 91838 57491
81657 27483 83858 28364 62726 26562 83759 27263 82827 27283
82858 47582 81837 28462 82837 58164 75748 58162 92000

BIBLIOGRAPHY

TRITHEIM (Johan). *Polygraphie et Universelle Écriture Cabalistique, traduit par Gabriel de Collange.* Paris, 1561.

BRIGHT (Timothy). *An Arte of Shorte, Swifte and Secret Writing by Character.* London, 1588.

SELENUS (Gustavus). *Cryptomenytics et Cryptographiac.* 1624.

ENGLAND (PARLIAMENT of). *The Charge of the Common Against Charles Stuart,* 1648.

CHARLES I. *Articles Exhibited Against the King.* 1648.

PORTA (Giovanni Baptista, della). *Natural Magick.* 1658.

de VIGÉNÈRE (Blaise). *Traité des chiffres.* 1670.

CARDANO (Girolamo). *Aphorismes d' Astrologie de Ptolomie, Hermes,* etc. 1657.

WILKINS (John, Bishop of Chester). *Mercury, or the Swifte Messenger.* 1694.

BACON (Francis). *Essays, or Councils, Moral and Civil.* 1720.

THICKNESSE (Phillip). *A Treatise on the Art of Deciphering.* 1772.

BACON (Francis). *Advancement of Learning.* 1772.

DAVYS (John). *An Essay on the Art of Decyphering.* 1737.

ASTLE (Thomas). *The Origin and Progress of Writing.* 1803.

HAMMER (Joseph). *Ancient Alphabets and Hieroglyphs Explained.* 1806.

KLEUBER (J. H.). *Kryptographik, L.*

REES (Abraham). W. Blair's Article on 'Cipher' in Cyclopædia or Universal Dictionary. 1819.

DALGARNO (George). *Ars Signorum.* 1834.

VESIN DE ROMANINI. *La Cryptographie dévoilée.* 1840.

—— *Résumé de la Cryptographie.* 1844.

MORSE (E. L.). *Samuel F. B. Morse, His Letters and Journals.*

MORSE (S. F. B.). *How to Learn Morse Alphabet in Half an Hour.* 1876.

KERCKOFF (Aug.). *La Cryptographie militaire.* 1883.

BEAUFORT. *Cryptography, a System of Secret Writing.* 1883.

JOSSE (H.). *La cryptographie et ses applications à l'art militaire.*

BRAILLE (LOUIS). *L'Écriture à l'usage des aveugles.* 1890.

PERRET (Paul Michel.) *Les règles de Cicco Simonetta pour le déchiffrement de 1474*. 1890.
BAZERIES (E.). *Chiffres Bazières*. 1893.
VALERIO (P.). *Cryptographie*. 1893.
SCHOOLING (J. H.). Article on Secret Writing in *Pall Mall Magazine*. 1896.
BAZERIES ET BU GAND. *La masque de fer*. 1893.
WATERS (W. G.). *Biographical Study of Jerome Cardano*. 1898.
GALLUP (E. W.). *Biliteral Cypher of Francis Bacon*. 1901.
BAZERIES (E.). *Les chiffres secrets devoilés*. 1901.
MAZZARINI (Cardinal). *Un agent secret de Mazarin*. 1904.
LEVY (Matthias). *William Shakespeare and Timothy Bright*. 1910.
FISKE (G. H.). *Studies of the Bilateral Cipher of Francis Bacon*. 1913.
MACBETH (J. C. H.). *The Marconi International Code*. 1920.
—— *Secret Ciphering for the Marconi International Code*. 1920.
BADEN-POWELL (Sir R. S. S.). *Aids to Scoutmastership*. 1920
LANGIE (A.). *Cryptography*. 1922.
FIGL (A.). *Système des chiffres*. 1926.
JACOT DE BOINOD ET COLLIER. *Marconi, Master of Space*. 1935.
MANSFIELD (L. C. S.). *The Solution of Codes and Ciphers*. 1936.

INDEX

	PAGE
A.B.C. Code	72, 78
Aegus	48
Aeneas Tacticus telegraph	14
African bush telegraph	56
Agamemnon	13, 48
Aids to deciphering	142
Aristagoras	14
Army cipher rules	99
Astles	8
Albam and Athbash	20
Auvray's cipher	94
Bacon, Francis	31, 35
Bartholdi, Baron	38
Balzac	68
Bazeries	40, 68
Bentley's code	78
Bible	8, 12, 19
Boy Scouts' signs	67
Braille	65
Brandenburg, Elector of	38
Bright, Dr. Timothy	85
British Army ciphers	96
Broglie, Duke of	32, 39
Brunswick-Luneberg, Duke of	32
Byrom, John	87
Cabbalism	12
Cardan, Jerome	27, 101
Cards, Marking of	60
Charlemagne	19

	PAGE
Charles I	36
Cicero	16
Cipher Wheel	106
Commercial codes	77
Cronfeld Substitution cipher	95
Cryptographic machines	116
Dalgarno, George, Hand alphabet of	66
Deaf and Dumb Alphabets	66, 67
Deciphering aids	142
Deciphering methods	121
Deciphering of Dictionary Codes	140
Dictionary codes	114
Egypt	8
Everett's shorthand	88
Figure or Numeral ciphers	113
Flag code	54
Fortius, Joachimus, Code of	48
Frederick III	38
French Army ciphers	94
Frequency tables	124
Gallup, Mrs.	35
German Army ciphers	90
Grand chiffre	40
Greene	35
Grille cipher	101
Gurney, Thomas	87

	PAGE
Hadrian	17
Hand alphabet	66, 67
Henry IV	37
Heraldry	51
Hermes	8
Invented alphabets	29, 34, 103, 135
Invisible inks	20
Iron Mask, Man in the	42
Jesuits	38
Jonson, Ben	36
Julius Caesar	13
Kipling, Rudyard	69
Lavater	28
Lloyds	70
Louis XIV, Cipher of	40
Machines, Cryptographic	116
Marconi	79, 80
Marlow	35
Mason marks	18
Mason's shorthand	87
Military codes and ciphers	89
Moon, Dr., Characters of	65
Morse	73
Moses	8, 13
Musical code	120
Napoleon's cipher	44
Nihilists' cipher	45
Numeral or Figure ciphers	113

	PAGE
Oghams	18
Pepys, Samuel	86
Periodic systems	108
Philostratus, Flavius	84
Pitman, Isaac, Shorthand of	87
Plato	8
Playfair	109
Plutarch	9
Poe, Edgar Allan	69
Polyalphabetic systems	105, 133
Polybius	15, 18, 48
Porta's code word cipher	30
Price code	62
Richelieu, Cardinal	39
Rohan, Chevalier de	121
Rowley, William	35
Russian cipher bureau	102
Semaphore alphabet	50
Selenus, Gustavus	32
Shakespeare	35
Shorthand	84
Ships' codes	48
Signals	49
Skytale	14
Sloan-Duplöyan shorthand	88
Soldiers' pocket book cipher	97
Solution of examples given	144
Solomon's alphabet	34
St. Cyr slide	94, 106
Syko	117

	PAGE		PAGE
Tacitus	14	Valeriano, Pietri	9
Tacticus, Aeneas, Telegraphic machine of	14	Vedas	8
		Vergennes' passport code	40
Tic Tac men	62	Verne, Jules	69
Tixère, Sieur de la	42, 44	Vigénère ciphers	31-33, 133, 136
Thompson, Sir Basil	92	Vigénère, Blaise de	31
Transpositions	19	Vimbois	42, 44
Transposition ciphers, deciphering of	135	Virgil	48
		Wallis, Dr.	36
Tramps' code	59	Webster's code	78
Transposition ciphers	104, 111	Whitelaw's telegraph code	73
Tritheim, John, Abbot	22	Wilkins, Bishop	7
Tritheim's code	23	Willis, John	86
Trojan war	13	Wolf, Father	38
Two-letter ciphers	129	Wolseley, Lord, cipher of	97
Types of codes and ciphers	103	Writing, Hieratic and demotic	8, 9
Tyro Tillius	16, 84	Zeus	8

Printed in Great Britain
by Amazon